10/8/15
$19.95

SHORTS AND BRIEFS

*A Collection of Short Plays
and Brief Principles of Playwriting*

Gregory Fletcher

Northampton House Press

PN
1661
.F55
2015

Northampton House e-edition, 2015, 978-1-937997-49-6.

Northampton House Press trade paper edition, 2015, ISBN 978-1-937997-50-2.

Library of Congress Control Number: 2014945676.

9 8 7 6 5 4 3 2

In memory of Matilde and Theodore Ferro

SHORTS AND BRIEFS

Contents

Introduction

When I won the National Ten-Minute Play Award from the Kennedy Center American College Theater Festival, the prize confirmed how much I connected to the short play format. I've been passionately writing, reading, and responding to them ever since. This collection of short plays and brief principles gives me the opportunity to share my own short plays as well as the knowledge I've gained over the years working within the genre.

I hope this collection of nine shorts and fifteen briefs will be of use to playwrights, producers, directors, actors, and, of course, students who are working within the genre. I also hope this collection will be of assistance to classes studying Playwriting, Play Analysis, Directing, Acting, and Introduction to Theater.

Directing students must understand the basics of playwriting and the vocabulary of a playwright. Since many directing opportunities involve working on new plays, directors must understand the craft of playwriting, its vocabulary, and how to offer notes for revisions. When collaboration between playwright and director flourishes, two careers can often launch together.

Acting students, too, must understand how much thought and work goes into writing a play, and consequently why the playwright's dialogue deserves to be memorized verbatim. In the same way that an actor cannot truly appreciate a stage manager until taking a stage management class, respect for playwrights is achieved when actors experience the playwriting process.

It's invaluable for Acting and Directing classes to work on short plays. Scene-work from full-length plays can often be one-note, with little forward development and few, if any, turning points. Short plays offer a beginning/middle/end and a full character arc. When a scene from a full-length is presented to the class, the back-story has to be explained so the scene makes sense; and/or, when the scene ends, there's little sense of completion because the play continues. An audience is left hanging as to what becomes of the characters and story. Short plays offer actors and directors the chance to work on a complete play that does not require any explanation or setup, and when the curtain falls, there's a sense of completion.

These plays and briefs may also be used for an Intro to Theatre class, which typically covers each aspect of a theatrical production: playwriting, directing, casting, acting, costumes, sets, lighting, sound, producing, stage management, and the critical review, etc. To examine such aspects of theater, full-length plays are usually read and scrutinized. Using a different full-length play for each aspect is impractical for a one-semester class. However, using a short play for each aspect requires minimal reading time, and the class will appreciate the variety of subjects and characters.

An ideal way to begin a Playwriting class is by studying and writing short plays. Once the student is able to identify the difference between a short play, a sketch, and a scene, it becomes very clear how much in common the short play has with the one-act and full-length, which then are the logical next steps. Writing the one-act or full-length play will be easier once the short play has been mastered.

Play Analysis is the process of examining the many components that make up a play. Dissecting short plays will be an easier first step before moving on to full-length plays. For mid-term and final examinations, short plays offer better time management for both the student and the professor. A full-length play would require a take-home exam, because it would be impossible to read and review a lengthy piece in one exam period. However, a short play can be read and reviewed with plenty of time left over to answer questions or write a critical essay.

I'm honored to be sharing my short plays and brief principles on playwriting. I can't think of anything more rewarding than helping support and inspire students of theater! My very best wishes to you, your work, and your success in the great genre of short plays.

Gregory Fletcher
New York City

The Shorts

Quick Summaries of the Short Plays

Eight Times Around
Cast size: 1 female and 1 male (30 years old)
A dramedy in which Garson is in between jobs, and time is running out. Returning to his placement agency for the seventh time, the interview is anything but typical, because this is not your usual placement agency. What Garson is offered only happens once in a lifetime.

Family of Flechner
Cast size: 2 males (18 years old and mid-20's)
Sebastian longs to be a member of the Family. He's convinced his Godfather Artie is a Godfather "in the life," and that a favor Sebastian has been asked to complete is a Mafia initiation. Lucky for Sebastian, he's Hungarian and not connected in the least, because the favor turns downright embarrassing. A comedy about yearning to belong.

Hangman
Cast size: 2 males (20's)
As Cliff rushes to a last minute temp job, he jumps into the last car of a local subway train without noticing the signs of "construction delays." When the train stops dead in between stations, Cliff is stranded with one other passenger. A stranger? A friend? A misunderstanding? Just when they think they know, subway hell changes these men's lives forever. A drama in tribute to LeRoy Jones and his play, *Dutchman.*

The Moon Alone
Cast size: 3 females (18 years old, late 20's, early 30's)
At midnight, two women try to mend a broken friendship, but it's not until they are accosted by a stranger that they're able to do so. A dramedy about the power of extended families.

The Nine-Month Fix
Cast size: 1 female (22 yrs. old) and 1 male (early 40's)
Steph is nine months pregnant, and today's the due date. And not just for the baby. Steph must right the wrong that threatened to tear apart her life and family. Instead of living as a victim, she tries to turn a negative to positive. A drama about second chances.

Not Tonight
Cast size: 1 female (40's) and 2 males (20's & 40's)
Bill returns home from a few years in the Afghan War to discover he's not the only wounded one in his family. A new war zone opens before him, and this time he's unprepared for battle. A drama.

Roast Beef and the Rare Kiss
Cast size: 2 females and 2 males (20's)
The perfect Friday evening: a double date with best friends, a delicious home-cooked meal, and a romantic film with popcorn on its way. The only thing more perfect is the kiss. A surprise kiss that comes out of nowhere, the kind of kiss one will always remember. That rare kiss that can never be mentioned or repeated ever again.

Robert Mapplethorpe's Flowers
Cast size: 2 males (50's)
In a long-term relationship, as things have slowed to a shallow crawl, Gary and Scott explore a unique approach to getting it back. A romantic comedy.

Stairway to Heaven

Cast size: 1 female (17 yrs. old) and 1 male (16 yrs. old)

An estranged teenage sister and brother struggle to connect as they consider the life they'll lead after the recent death of their father. A coming of age dramedy.

For performance licensing rights, *Stairway to Heaven* is licensed by Dramatic Publishing at www.dramaticpublishing.com. For the other short plays in this collection, a reduced royalty rate is available, either for individual plays or for a package of six to eight plays. For performance licensing rights, please contact the playwright at www.gregoryfletcher.com.

Eight Times Around
a short play
a dramedy

by Gregory Fletcher

CAST OF CHARACTERS:

PLACEMENT OFFICER, female, appears to be around 30 years old, in business attire, speaks many languages, a people person.

GARSON, male, appears to be around 30 years old, wearing a shirt and tie because he thinks it's expected at an interview.

Premiered in New York City by Emerging Artists Theatre, artistic director Paul Adams, directed by Rebecca Kendall, featuring Laura Fois and Ryan Hilliard.

SETTING: A business cubicle in a high rise building.

AT RISE: GARSON stands at a window, admiring the view. PLACEMENT OFFICER enters.

PLACEMENT OFFICER: Running a little late. Hello. Which language do you speak?

GARSON: What?

PLACEMENT OFFICER: Right. Any preferred dialect? Whichever you like. *(Using an East Texan accent)* Shoot, I been doin' East Texas all mornin' long and my head is fixin' to bust, let me tell you. *(Using a British accent)* Perhaps British, if you don't mind? I say, isn't it simply marvelous what a little dialect change can do?

GARSON: Ever get tired of this?

PLACEMENT OFFICER: Indeed. That last interview almost did me in. Cup of tea?

GARSON: Oh, no, just want to get this over with, if you don't mind.

PLACEMENT OFFICER: Yes, of course. Been waiting long?

GARSON: Don't really know. My watch stopped. A couple days? Maybe a week?

PLACEMENT OFFICER: Oh, dear me. Sorry.

GARSON: But it's a very comfortable...cubicle and, man oh man, what a view. Breathtaking.

PLACEMENT OFFICER: It is glorious, isn't it? Yes, just lovely. Pity those who allow themselves to get so busy, they forget to notice. Tah luv. Well. Shall we? *(She sits behind her desk and indicates a chair for Garson.)*

GARSON: I was hoping for a little more time.

PLACEMENT OFFICER: Haven't heard that one before, have I? But you only get so much time and then it's back to work. That's life. Or some call it unemployment. *(A big laugh.)* I love saying that. Sorry. *(She refers to her smart phone.)* Yes, Garson, I remember you.

GARSON: It's only my...I don't know, too often? I mean, is there a limit to how many times I can come back here?

PLACEMENT OFFICER: As many times as it takes.

GARSON: I don't mean to be difficult.

PLACEMENT OFFICER: Don't be silly, it takes all kinds; we know that to be true.

GARSON: Yes, well, you've been very helpful in the past.

PLACEMENT OFFICER: It's my pleasure. And I have no doubt that this time we can find the perfect—

GARSON: I'd like something outdoorsy.

PLACEMENT OFFICER: Well, that's a big change from the casino.

GARSON: Yes, cooped up all day in a locked office with no windows, and cameras in every corner, just counting and counting. And for what?

PLACEMENT OFFICER: Yes, very good.

GARSON: I was dying to get out of there; I'm glad it happened. I mean, I would've stuck it out, don't get me wrong.

PLACEMENT OFFICER: But everything works out as needed. Excellent.

GARSON: So if I could get back to the horse farm again.

PLACEMENT OFFICER: Oh.

GARSON: It'll be better this time; I know exactly what to do now.

PLACEMENT OFFICER: Too much scenery and down time, I'm afraid.

GARSON: But I was good with the horses, no complaints there.

PLACEMENT OFFICER: None, but I'm thinking something a little bit more structured and...urban might best suit your needs. I'm not even sure the horse farm is still around. Highly doubt it. Any other thoughts at all?

GARSON: Huh?

PLACEMENT OFFICER: Right.

GARSON: Maybe if I could see my file, I'd have a better idea of what I'm doing wrong.

PLACEMENT OFFICER: I wouldn't look at it so black and white if I were you. Everyone has his or her own pace.

GARSON: But my pace seems like it's getting slower and slower. I'm not a young man anymore.

PLACEMENT OFFICER: Why, you don't look a day over thirty.

GARSON: Thirty! I wish. What I'd give to just stay at home.

PLACEMENT OFFICER: Yes, getting home, it's lovely to verbalize your goal. And that's exactly it, isn't it?

GARSON: But if you could give me some...anything so I won't have to come back here again and keep bothering you.

PLACEMENT OFFICER: I assure you, the things you learn, you do carry on. May not seem like it, but it does get easier with each new placement. The question is, how do you see yourself getting it done?

GARSON: I can take the criticism, just tell me. No one ever says anything, and then I'm back here starting over...Jesus Christ.

PLACEMENT OFFICER: Oh, now, don't blame Him.

GARSON: Yeah, where is He when you need Him?

PLACEMENT OFFICER: I believe He's teaching a master class at the moment. *(Another big laugh)* I love saying that. Sorry. Let's take a look, shall we?

GARSON: The thought of another placement; I...I don't know if I have it in me. I was so close to retiring. Two more years and I would have been in Florida taking it easy. Sitting on the beach, watching the young people, the sunsets—

PLACEMENT OFFICER: Sounds like another horse farm, if you ask me. Been there, done that.

GARSON: But just to wake up one morning to fall flat on my face? I can't believe I signed up for that.

PLACEMENT OFFICER: You have made some nice big strides, and everyone gets to this point, believe me.

GARSON: But it never gets easier? It's like I'm being set up to fail.

PLACEMENT OFFICER: Some say, this frustration, it's a good sign. The last hurdle, if you will. Of course, it's up to you, yes?

GARSON: I know it when I'm sitting across from you, but it just goes out of my head with each new placement. Everything does.

PLACEMENT OFFICER: Some things can't be given away; we have to earn them. I know what you're going through; I've been on the other side of this desk.

GARSON: Yeah right, how many times, once?

PLACEMENT OFFICER: Five. That's right, five. Could've done it in four maybe, but I got mixed up and...lost a few decades. But then I got back on track. And...voilà.

GARSON: Wow. I wouldn't have...you look good.

PLACEMENT OFFICER: We've got an amazing perks package here; I've had some work done. And that's not the half of it, with love exuding from every breath, every moment, every thing. Not to mention the desserts. To die for. And there's no pollution, no regrets, no acid reflux. I could go on and on, but you'll see, when you're finally home. You'll kick yourself for taking so long to figure it out. You can do it, Garson. Here, want to see? *(She offers her hand, and Garson takes it. As they look into each other's eyes, Garson fights back the tears.)*

GARSON: It's love, isn't it? Pure openhearted love...that's what I've been...I'm gonna do it this time, I really am. Yes, I feel younger than ever! My God, look at my hands. Like a young man's. Let's do it! What do you have for me?

PLACEMENT OFFICER: Yes, very good, that's the spirit. *(Refers to her smart phone.)* All right, here's something. Needs to be filled immediately. Could be a good match. Yes, how would you like to be a female born in the Bronx with only forty-five minutes of labor?

GARSON: You got to be kidding me. The Bronx?

PLACEMENT OFFICER: Of course if we can't fill it, we'll have to miscarry.

GARSON: Don't try to guilt me into it. It's still got to be what's best for me, right?

PLACEMENT OFFICER: I can promise you this, there'll be no alcoholic parents this time or sibling rivalry. The only thing I see is a minor car accident. Oh, and what's this?

GARSON: Yeah, thought so.

PLACEMENT OFFICER: The death of a best friend. That'll be hard. But other than that, you should be able to accomplish what you need.

GARSON: But the Bronx?

PLACEMENT OFFICER: What if I can make you extra pretty? Shall I check upstairs?

GARSON: It won't matter with that accent. And the cold winters, that fast pace, it'll be Atlantic City all over again. No, I definitely want something more southern.

PLACEMENT OFFICER: Alright, it's good to know what you want, let's keep looking. Ah, here's an opening in Lima. A boy with three older adoring sisters and lots of pets. Looks lovely, shall we?

GARSON: Keep scrolling.

PLACEMENT OFFICER: Scrolling, scrolling...oh.

GARSON: I knew it.

PLACEMENT OFFICER: One leg is shorter than the other.

GARSON: There goes team sports.

PLACEMENT OFFICER: By the time team sports matter, you'll be twelve and home alone for the first time; you won't know what hits you.

GARSON: Come again?

PLACEMENT OFFICER: A fireball from the sky. Destroys the entire house. For what it's worth, you'll be the leading story worldwide.

GARSON: To live through that?

PLACEMENT OFFICER: You won't have to.

GARSON: Oh, my poor parents. My three adoring sisters! Do they know? They actually chose these lives?

PLACEMENT OFFICER: *(Showing the screen on her smart phone)* Look, they're getting your room ready as we speak.

GARSON: I don't know, I'm not trying to be impossible here. But my gut is saying let someone else grab it.

PLACEMENT OFFICER: Listening to one's gut is a major tool to getting things accomplished. Keep listening.

GARSON: And three adoring sisters sound very distracting. Sounds fun though. Not the fireball but...never mind.

PLACEMENT OFFICER: Here's something just posted. Yes, a similar situation but female and a longer life. Let's see where. Scrolling, scrolling...Texas. Shit. Well, hold on, it's Dallas.

GARSON: Is there a difference?

PLACEMENT OFFICER: Of course there is. Let's see, catastrophes? None.

GARSON: Impossible.

PLACEMENT OFFICER: And you'll have thirty-six years. That should be plenty of time. Oh, look how pretty. And popular. And... *(She stops but covers her true reactions.)* Trust me, this one's going fast.

GARSON: Thirty-six years is enough? *(No response)* You sure?

PLACEMENT OFFICER: I'm sorry, what? Yes, of course, why waste all those years growing old when you can be home? Right?

GARSON: How does it end?

PLACEMENT OFFICER: You better grab this one while you can.

GARSON: How does it end?

PLACEMENT OFFICER: Why worry yourself?

GARSON: It's bad, isn't it? I can tell. I want to see.

PLACEMENT OFFICER: *(Reluctantly allows Garson to view the smart phone.)* Just touch the arrow.

GARSON: *(He touches the smart phone and slowly sickens with disgust.)* Why are those boys...? Oh, no. No. How could they?

PLACEMENT OFFICER: It happens a lot faster than it seems.

GARSON: You don't call this a catastrophe?

PLACEMENT OFFICER: Once you're in the coma, it's over. You're gone.

GARSON: Why does anyone volunteer to be one of those sickos?

PLACEMENT OFFICER: It's all part of the process. We're hoping it'll be a major turning point for at least two of them. All four, maybe. It's only their first time around. I can keep looking, if you like.

GARSON: And you're saying, up to that last moment, there're no distractions?

PLACEMENT OFFICER: It does feel like a good match; I'm not just saying so. This could be it, Garson.

GARSON: What's her name?

PLACEMENT OFFICER: Sharon.

GARSON: 'Cause I want to do it this time...all the way. Not isolated and alone, but loving. And what was the other thing? Yes, listening to my gut. Please God, let me remember this time. He doesn't make it easy, does He. Then, finally, I'll be home. Six times around.

PLACEMENT OFFICER: Seven actually, but who's counting.

GARSON: Seven times around.

PLACEMENT OFFICER: Yes.

GARSON: Yes.

PLACEMENT OFFICER: If you're ready, just touch where indicated.

GARSON: *(He touches the smart phone.)* May I have one more look? *(Garson returns to the window, nervous with what's to come.)*

PLACEMENT OFFICER: *(She joins him as they admire the glorious view.)* You're going to be fine.

GARSON: I'll be fine when I have such a view.

PLACEMENT OFFICER: And you will. *(Touching his shoulder)* You're shaking.

GARSON: You bet your ass. No disrespect.

PLACEMENT OFFICER: I understand. Shall we? *(Garson agrees. Placement Officer sends a text message from her smart phone. White light slowly floods the cubicle.)*

GARSON: *(Quietly)* Be home soon?

END OF PLAY

(As a reminder, a reduced royalty rate is available, either for individual plays or for a package of six to eight plays. For performance licensing rights, please contact the playwright at www.gregoryfletcher.com)

Family of Flechner
a short play
a comedy

by Gregory Fletcher

CAST OF CHARACTERS:

ARTIE, male, 26 years old, intimidating, has lived in New York City since his late teens and speaks with a noticeable Hungarian accent.

SEBASTIAN, male, 18 years old, a bit simple, has lived in New York City since his early childhood and speaks with a New York street accent without any trace of his Hungarian roots.

Finalist for America's Short Play Festival at City Theatre in Miami.

PLACE: New York City, the East 80's.

SETTING: Artie's basement studio, little to no sunlight, shadows, sparse, a man-cave. Besides the front door, there is a table and chairs with a low hanging light.

AT RISE: ARTIE paces. The intercom buzzes near the front door.

ARTIE: So help me, Sebastian. *(He pushes a button on the intercom.)* I'm gonna—you—if you—I'm telling you—hang him by his—don't you tell me—you—by his thumbs—I mean it—lousy sorry excuse for a... *(There's a timid knock at the door, and Artie opens the door and pulls Sebastian inside. He looks to see if the coast is clear, then slams and locks the door. SEBASTIAN is 18 years old and dressed like an old time Mafia gangster with a dark overcoat he holds closed in front.)* Damn it, Sebastian, I thought my instructions were very clear!

SEBASTIAN: Uh...excuse me, Godfather?

ARTIE: What the hell you wearing? Is this what you wore? Never mind, Sebastian, just get over here and put it on the table!

SEBASTIAN: Uh...you said you wouldn't call me that no more.

ARTIE: You know what time it is? Where you been for crying out loud?

SEBASTIAN: My name. You promised. If I did this job.

ARTIE: I shouldn't call you your name? You always been Sebastian.

SEBASTIAN: *(Covering his ears)* La-la-la, la-la-la.

ARTIE: What do I care; let's see it, right now, let's go!

SEBASTIAN: I'm a Flechner like you. "You're your mother's son!" How many times did you scream it?

ARTIE: And your mother's name is...?

SEBASTIAN: Aza.

ARTIE: Her *last* name.

SEBASTIAN: Flechner. Like you.

ARTIE: It's Lipka!

SEBASTIAN: Not before she married, "which she never should've done!" How many times did you scream it?

ARTIE: Stop busting my balls, Sebastian, I never once said anything—

SEBASTIAN: *(Covering his ears again)* La-la-la, la-la-la.

ARTIE: I've got people waiting. You know how late you are?!

SEBASTIAN: The job is done. The initiation, complete.

ARTIE: Huh? What the hell you talking? You mean this little favor?

SEBASTIAN: Who gets paid for a favor? What's my job rate anyway?

ARTIE: You don't have a job rate, and you'll get your money when I get mine. Now, let's see it! Sebastian, now!

SEBASTIAN: Sebastian is dead, I told you! Sorry. Didn't mean to match your fury.

ARTIE: If Sebastian's dead, then he's dead. May he rest in peace. So whoever you are, where is it? 'Cuz I don't see it nowheres.

SEBASTIAN: Death and rebirth. That's all I'm saying. But I didn't mean no disrespect, especially to the family.

ARTIE: To who? Who is this "family?"

SEBASTIAN: Who else I got? My father's run out of town. And my mother, executed.

ARTIE: Shut up with the...shut up, you, just zip it. You know your father ran off with some girl half his age. And trust me, we're all still very perplexed about it. And your mother, she died of cancer. Ovarian cancer to be exact. In fact, it's a universal problem, nothing special.

SEBASTIAN: But Godfather—

ARTIE: And stop calling me.... I am your uncle, you hear me? Just an uncle, that's it, take it or leave it. We clear?

SEBASTIAN: But you always been my Godfather.

ARTIE: I am too young to be your friggin' Godfather.

SEBASTIAN: Since my christening.

ARTIE: Oh, I was at your christening? How you know that?

SEBASTIAN: I got the DVD.

ARTIE: There was no one else; they told me, stand there; they thought it was...what do I know; I was five years old!

SEBASTIAN: Please, Godfather, this day is very special to me.

ARTIE: Your christening?

SEBASTIAN: No, *today*. The chance, a job, to be part of the "family."

ARTIE: What did I tell you about the "family?"

SEBASTIAN: Okay, "capeesh," I capeesh.

ARTIE: Is that supposed to be Italian? We're friggin' Hungarian! Not "in the family" or connected or even acquainted. I swear to God, I'm gonna throw out the entire box set of *The Sopranos* if I hear this talk one more time! We never even been to Jersey! Now, put it on the table before I bust a vein. I swear on my sister's grave, you don't have it, do you? Is that what this is about? You screwed it up; I should'a known.

SEBASTIAN: Course I got it; I can be trusted. We're family.

ARTIE: *(He grabs Sebastian and pulls out a pocket comb and puts it up to Sebastian's head, as if it were a gun.)* I gave you a chance, and you blow it? Is that what happened?

SEBASTIAN: You're only making it worse.

ARTIE: I'm counting to three!

SEBASTIAN: Roughing me up only makes it worse.

ARTIE: One!

SEBASTIAN: The feel of the cold steel. The smell of the powder—

ARTIE: Two!

SEBASTIAN: I have it; it's on my person. I just can't get it at the moment.

ARTIE: What are you...? What the...? *(Sebastian indicates his crotch.)* It's...there? Down there? You did not. Down there?

SEBASTIAN: 'Cause you said it's worth thousands.

ARTIE: So you put it down there?

SEBASTIAN: You said no pockets, to wear it.

ARTIE: On an ankle! Around a bicep. But down there?

SEBASTIAN: I took a shower; I'm fresh.

ARTIE: My exact words, "wear it tight up against you so it can't fall off."

SEBASTIAN: I did. It can't.

ARTIE: So you lost it? Of course you lost it!

SEBASTIAN: Don't think so.

ARTIE: A jiggle here, a jiggle there, right out your pant leg!

SEBASTIAN: Nope. Snug as a bug, that's the problem.

ARTIE: Huh?

SEBASTIAN: It's so tight, it's practically cutting into me.

ARTIE: Huh?

SEBASTIAN: I meditated, chanted, prayed, everything but sit in a bathtub of cold water. Are diamonds waterproof?

ARTIE: Huh?

SEBASTIAN: I thought about going to the Emergency room, but what if they called the cops? Or what if a nurse takes a photo, and I end up on YouTube and go viral! *(Artie throws Sebastian across the table and shoves his hand down Sebastian's pants.)* Being rough won't help, Uncle Artie, that tickles. Not helping, not helping. *(Artie pulls his hand out with amazement.)* See? What I tell you? Now, you believe me, Uncle Artie?

ARTIE: I am not...you are not my family! *(Indicating Sebastian's crotch) Clearly*, you are not *my* family. A *Lipka*, maybe, Christ, no wonder your father...with that girl half his age. No wonder a lot. How long has it been up like that?

SEBASTIAN: Since the job. Just as he was being lowered into the grave, I high-tailed it over to the house, just like you said. When the coast was clear, I wandered upstairs to his room, second door on the right, dresser on the left, third drawer down, hidden in the back, inside a brown paper bag. Do I follow instructions or what? And it was so sparkling beautiful. I never held nothing so...in all my life. That's when I started tingling all over; I couldn't believe this day was finally here. My big break. Then I heard people arriving downstairs and I thought, what if someone sees me coming out and tries to rough me up or search me, 'cause everybody's always picking on me. And I didn't know where to hide it so...since I was...up for the job, I fastened it. And it wasn't going anywhere. So I went downstairs, ate some stuffed eggs, some golabki, some more stuffed eggs, and I was out of there. Having completed my first job. Very excited to say the least. To say the least 'cause it kept getting tighter. I didn't think I'd make it here in one piece, so I stopped home to...to—

ARTIE: You take them small blue pills or something?

SEBASTIAN: No, nothing.

ARTIE: It's mental conditioning, that's all. I used to talk myself down all the time. Okay, listen. Forget about everything. The job, the diamonds, your girth. Just let it all go. Now, think about something...disgusting. Like your babysitter, remember?

SEBASTIAN: You?

ARTIE: When I was at school! What was her name? The one with the red rash down her neck.

SEBASTIAN: Sister Yana?

ARTIE: Yeah, picture her giving you a bath. Her hands, the soap, your naked body in a tub that only has an inch of water. And she's butt naked.

SEBASTIAN: Without her headpiece? She never takes that off.

ARTIE: And that red rash is two inches from your face; you see it?

SEBASTIAN: It was a birthmark, not a rash. She called it a Holy Communion wine stain.

ARTIE: And you're smelling her breath. What is it, cabbage?

SEBASTIAN: Velveeta.

ARTIE: And she always had something stuck in her teeth.

SEBASTIAN: Wonder bread.

ARTIE: She was always...what was she always muttering?

SEBASTIAN: The multiplication table. No nun can multiply like Sister Yana.

ARTIE: Now feel her hot Velvetta breath hitting you in the face. *Two* times *two* equals *four*. *Two* times *three* equals *six*. And the water's cold. *Three* times *three* equals nine. What else did she do that made you cringe?

SEBASTIAN: Playing the autoharp. How she could go on.

ARTIE: What was her favorite song?

SEBASTIAN: "Smoke on the Water."
DUM DUM DUM.
DUM-DUM DA-DUM.
DUM DUM DUM.
DUM-DUM.

ARTIE: Here's the one that always worked for me. Never failed. *(Quietly sings)*
JESUS LOVES THE LITTLE CHILDREN
ALL THE CHILDREN OF THE WORLD

RED AND YELLOW, BLACK AND WHITE
THEY ARE PRECIOUS IN HIS SIGHT
JESUS LOVES THE LITTLE CHILDREN OF THE WORLD.

ARTIE & SEBASTIAN:
JESUS LOVES THE LITTLE CHILDREN
ALL THE CHILDREN OF THE WORLD
RED AND YELLOW, BLACK AND WHITE
THEY ARE PRECIOUS IN HIS SIGHT *(Harmonizing)*
JESUS LOVES THE LITTLE CHILDREN OF THE WORLD.

SEBASTIAN: Wow, you did it; you did it! *(Sebastian puts his hand down his pants, pulls out a diamond bracelet, and gives it to Artie.)*

ARTIE: That's it. That's the one. Thank you, Grandpa Max. For all you did for me. Even now with this. Until we meet again.

SEBASTIAN: He saved all your e-mails, you know? Printed out, all stacked in the same drawer with the bracelet, which had your name on it by the way.

ARTIE: Not like they'd give it to me.

SEBASTIAN: But he was your grandpa; everyone knew it.

ARTIE: Not legally. Not when it comes to money like this. But now, his will be done. Thanks to you. Hey, when I'm back, I'll fix all your favorites to celebrate.

SEBASTIAN: Kielbasa?

ARTIE: And hunter's stew.

SEBASTIAN: And wild boar?

ARTIE: You never had wild boar in your life.

SEBASTIAN: It was mom's favorite. No?

ARTIE: Yes. Our mother's specialty. But nothing like it here, believe me. Hey, I got three words for you. Good job, Sebastian. Jeez, sorry, what am I supposed to call you?

SEBASTIAN: What am I supposed to call *you*?

ARTIE: Why not Artie like everybody else?

SEBASTIAN: Godfather Artie?

ARTIE: It's embarrassing. Look it, say we just be brothers; I always wanted a kid brother and you...well...this way, you're a Flechner like me. Deal? *(Suddenly, Sebastian embraces Artie.)* Okay. Okay-okay. Okay. Okay. *(Artie realizes how much Sebastian means to him and embraces him back tightly, a bonding moment. After a moment, they part and nod.)* So. Angelo Flechner. How's that? You like it? Sounds good. *(Sebastian agrees.)* Then sit tight. *(Artie exits; Sebastian beams with pride.)*

<u>END OF PLAY</u>

(As a reminder, a reduced royalty rate is available, either for individual plays or for a package of six to eight plays. For performance licensing rights, please contact the playwright at <u>www.gregoryfletcher.com</u>)

Hangman
a short play
a drama

by Gregory Fletcher

—in tribute to LeRoi Jones (aka Amiri Baraka) and his play
Dutchman—

CAST OF CHARACTERS:

CLIFF, male, late 20's, out of work New York actor, dressed
corporate for a temp job, educated, articulate, outgoing, secure, in-
shape.

NICKY, male, late 20's, a salesman, very handsome, gym body,
married with a wife and kids, persuasive, outgoing, confident,
cocky, ultimately dangerous.

Premiered in workshop at Edward Albee's Last Frontier Theater
Conference in Valdez, Alaska. Premiered in production in
Provincetown at the Provincetown Theatre Company's &
Narrowland Arts' Festival of New Plays, featuring Eric Dray and
Andres Branger. Then produced by Boston's Another Country
Productions, artistic director Lyralen Kaye, featuring Chris Reed &
Marlon Smith-Jones.

TIME: 1990's

SETTING: The last car of a subway train.

AT RISE: NICKY is sitting alone, waiting. Nicky is dressed for the
gym in shorts and a sports-oriented sweat-shirt. His gym bag is
next to him on the empty row of seats. Just as the subway doors
close, CLIFF jumps inside. Cliff is dressed in a suit with a red

ribbon pinned to his lapel. He carries a book-bag and the Arts
section to *The New York Times*.

CLIFF: Yes! Thank God! That was close. *(Cliff takes a seat,
and Nicky pulls a banana from his gym bag, peels it, slowly moves
it to his mouth, and takes a bite. Cliff watches but when they meet
eyes, he opens his newspaper. Nicky pulls another banana from his
gym bag and offers it.)* That's okay, thanks anyway. Too many
carbs. Just teasing, not me, I've got this friend. He won't eat
anything that's...it's very complicated...takes all the fun out of
breakfast. Eating. Life. Never mind.

NICKY: *(Indicating the newspaper)* Sports?

CLIFF: No, Arts.

NICKY: *(He puts his foot up; Cliff notices that he can see up
Nicky's pant leg.)* Do I look familiar or something?

CLIFF: No, I...believe me, I'd remember.

NICKY: 'Cause you made a face like...I could swear you
recognized me.

CLIFF: No, it's just...I can see your...would you mind not...

NICKY: What?

CLIFF: Well, you're...I can see your...never mind.

NICKY: *(Adjusting himself)* Oh, I'm sorry. How's that? Better?
(Embarrassed, Cliff doesn't want to look.) Can you see me or not?
The view. How is the view?

CLIFF: You're fine. *(Nicky stands up on the row of seats quite
close to Cliff with his crotch at eye level.)* What're you doing?

NICKY: *(Tossing the peel out the upper window)* Littering.
You're not gonna turn me in, are you? *(Cliff moves to another seat.
Nicky stretches and drops his hands to the floor. As Nicky catches
Cliff watching, Cliff quickly returns to his paper.)* Why don't you

put the paper down and stop pretending. Nothing to be ashamed of. Yep, I can always tell.

CLIFF: Maybe you need to work on *telling* when it's appropriate or not. And waiting for mutual consent. Flashing yourself to the wrong guy could get you in a lot of trouble.

NICKY: You speaking from experience?

CLIFF: Are you always so...? That's what I hate about you good-looking guys. You get away with whatever you want; everyone wants to kiss up and give-give-give.

NICKY: Including you? Bingo.

CLIFF: No, I...I'm not that type. Sorry.

NICKY: I'd say you are.

CLIFF: Well then, you're not *my* type, how's that?

NICKY: Ouch. But you keep looking. You shaved too fast this morning. You woke up hearing your temp agency beg you to accept a last minute job. And, hey, no auditions today so perfect timing, right? What with the rent coming up. So you jumped into this corporate look from your closet and grabbed a high protein banana muffin with no carbs. Now you're hauling your ass downtown to word-process and answer phones, only you missed the express train and grabbed the local instead, not noticing the sign about construction delays. *(The train screeches to a stop, surrounded by darkness outside the windows.)* And here we are. In the last car. So what's your name? No, let me guess. How many letters? I'll take an S.

CLIFF: You really get away with this?

NICKY: What?

CLIFF: You know exactly what.

NICKY: I hope you don't think I'm...seriously, I'm not that type.

CLIFF: What type?

NICKY: You know what type. I tried it once with a frat brother. We were both drunk. I couldn't get into it. *(Showing off his wedding ring.)* And I've been happily married ever since.

CLIFF: You used to be able to slip it on and off. But you pop your knuckles. So for the last, what, three or four years, you've been stuck with it. Unable to hide the fact that you're "happily" married with a wife and, how many, two little girls? Yeah, I know your type as well. Cocky, confident, you parade around the locker room all proud of what you got. Taking longer than anyone else to get dressed, giving all interested parties plenty of time to take you in. And you're even more generous in the steam room. Sitting there, wanting a release after your long hard workout. Meeting eyes with the guy next to you, looking down at yourself, then back to his eyes again. If he's still looking then you've made a catch. Or as you like to say, "Bingo." You pull your towel up to your face, pretending to wipe off the sweat, exposing yourself, pleased that he's still watching and growing. And even more strange, since you're not "that type at all," you're growing, too.

NICKY: Why don't you sit over here?

CLIFF: Because right now, I'm on my way to work and I'm wearing my best suit from Barney's, and it's not like I can hike it up over my head.

NICKY: There are other things we can do.

CLIFF: No, there's not; there is absolutely nothing here we can do.

NICKY: If you believe that, you're a discredit to your community.

CLIFF: What in the...?! How...?! You...?! No, let's not even talk. I'm just gonna... *(He takes a deep breath.)* And try to...unbelievable.

NICKY: You're the one who said I was good-looking and always get what I want.

CLIFF: Well, I hate to be the one to break your record but...no, actually, I don't mind being the one, this is sort of fun.

NICKY: Just being friendly. This is the thanks I get?

CLIFF: Rejection isn't something you're used to, is it?

NICKY: You must admit I have a great smile.

CLIFF: You're panicking.

NICKY: Irresistible, some say.

CLIFF: Just try to breathe into the pain.

NICKY: I don't see why we can't have some fun.

CLIFF: What do I look like to you?

NICKY: What do I look like to you? *(Cliff moves away, and Nicky tries again.)* Hey, I'm cool with you, and you're cool with me. *(Cliff gives him a look to suggest differently.)* Seriously, I'm cool with you and your boyfriend holding hands in public. With you and your domestic partner's license. Hell, I'm even cool with you adopting unwanted babies, why not? I like your type because your type understands gentrification and I like what you're doing to your community. You know, making it less flamboyant. It makes it a lot easier for us to mix. Hey, did I tell you, my wife and I saw *Angels In America*?

CLIFF: Wow, you're really up on things.

NICKY: And I see your movies when my wife wants to, your prime time invasion, you guys are all over the place. I told you, I had a queer fraternity brother, right? I didn't turn him in or get him kicked out or beat up. We were friends.

CLIFF: And I bet you got serviced whenever you wanted. *(Nicky smiles as if to agree.)* What am I thinking? I mean, you're gorgeous, a washboard stomach I bet, right? *(Nicky shows off his stomach.)* Love it. Buff arms, a beautiful head of hair, great legs, I've seen the package. Man, you've got it all.

NICKY: And I can be fast, too, no problem.

CLIFF: You can? Perfect. To be down on my knees right now, oh yeah, thank God you nailed my type. What was it, the red ribbon? The Arts section? Because I admitted you were handsome? And then, crazily enough, I panic; I don't know why. I mean, let's say this was a bar. God knows I've been hot and horny before and walked in, ordered a drink, and started up a conversation with a guy, and sooner than later—

NICKY: That's all I been saying.

CLIFF: It's so much easier between guys, isn't it? Funny thing is, I usually try not to blow crazy people. I'm not inferring that you're a lunatic! But you're just where I draw the line. So game's over. You lose. But hey, as a consolation prize, I'll give you some good advice, man to man. Try a bar. If you get out at 23rd, 18th, or Christopher, you'll have plenty to choose from. You should have no problem.

NICKY: What do you take me for?

CLIFF: Oh, don't tell me you're afraid of being seen going in or out?

NICKY: You're quick to judge.

CLIFF: Aren't the wife and kids tucked away on Long Island somewhere? Who's gonna see? You're safe.

NICKY: One might think you're trying to start something here.

CLIFF: Me? Me?!

NICKY: Am I wrong?

CLIFF: I'm not the one offering bananas!

NICKY: Take a breath. Settle down.

CLIFF: Get away from me. I'm fine! Just—

NICKY: You're upset, I'm sorry. If it's my fault, I apologize. You've had a hard life, I know. Growing up alone, isolated, feeling abnormal; you had no role models or anyone to talk to.

CLIFF: Oh please, you read someone's book or something?

NICKY: Your school friends shunned you, and the church too of course, that's a given. And your father, you never got along, not to mention your two or three attempted suicides as a teenager.

CLIFF: Is this Greg Louganis?

NICKY: Say whatever you want, but I understand you.

CLIFF: You don't know one thing about me, you freak. I come from a very close, supportive, loving family, and I was very popular in high school. I was runner-up "Most Friendly." And except for the occasional fag joke and the fact that my civil rights don't equal yours, I'm okay. Not ecstatic, but okay. But what I don't need is some breeder man pretending to cruise me, pretending to know me, pretending to like me, when all you really want is to get off.

NICKY: Jesus Christ, it used to be so much more simple. Alright, I know. It's a bumper sticker, five words. Give me a letter; it'll be fun.

CLIFF: It's not gonna be fun, trust me.

NICKY: Everyone loves this game.

CLIFF: Everyone is sick of your games.

NICKY: Okay, I'll give you an easy one...guess my name, five letters.

CLIFF: Listen...Bubba, this thing you're doing here, this hobby of yours, it's over. Dated. Give it up.

NICKY: You know, whatever your name is—Steve, Bruce, Liberace—you're starting to get on my nerves.

CLIFF: Then why don't you stop cruising me? And better yet, go back to your happily married wife and see if *she'll* blow you. Or is she sick of you, too?

NICKY: At least I have a wife.

CLIFF: A beard! A showpiece!

NICKY: You calling me a faggot?

CLIFF: And how alone and empty she must feel.

NICKY: Acting all high and mighty.

CLIFF: Can you even get it up for her?

NICKY: Pretending to know me?

CLIFF: Who's pretending to know whom?

NICKY: Just make your move!

CLIFF: End this game!

NICKY: You.

CLIFF: You!

NICKY: You!

CLIFF: Why? Why me? Why me!

NICKY: I'm sorry.

CLIFF: You're what?

NICKY: Sorry. I'm sorry.

CLIFF: Sorry?

NICKY: Yeah. I mean it. Sorry. Really. Okay?

CLIFF: So then...as long as it's...over. Yeah? You sure?

NICKY: It is. Thanks. I don't know why I...shake? Please.

CLIFF: It's not necessary. If I could just...and you...

NICKY: Sometimes, I just need to shake to calm down. Seriously, that's all. *(Cliff reluctantly shakes his hand.)* That's better. Calming down. Whew. Thanks.

CLIFF: Can I have my hand back?

NICKY: Oh. Yeah, sure. You remember how we used to get hugs to calm us down? That was nice. People today don't hug. You know what I mean? Hugs?

CLIFF: You're not telling me, you need a...a hug? Awkward.

NICKY: You think? No, of course not. Well, if you're offering.

CLIFF: I wasn't.

NICKY: I'm teasing.

CLIFF: Good. What a relief.

NICKY: Well...you want?

CLIFF: Not really.

NICKY: Like you don't need a hug, too?

CLIFF: Who are you now, my mother?

NICKY: Come on.

CLIFF: Oh, Geez Louise. *(He reluctantly allows Nicky to embrace him. After a moment, Cliff feels something at Nicky's lower back and suddenly pulls a knife from Nicky's shorts. Nicky tries to grab for it, and Cliff pulls it on Nicky.)* What the—?

NICKY: What're you...? Give it. I said—

CLIFF: *(Swinging the knife to keep Nicky away.)* Oh my God! Were you...? Were you gonna...?

NICKY: Careful. Slow down. Easy.

CLIFF: Answer me!

NICKY: Maybe games don't end without a winner.

CLIFF: Get away from me! Or I'll...

NICKY: Or what! Show me. Win or lose. *(Neither moves. A tense moment.)*

END OF PLAY

The Moon Alone
a short play
a dramedy

by Gregory Fletcher

CAST OF CHARACTERS:

PRECIOUS, female, 30's, plain, almost sloppy, comfortably dressed.

SAMANTHA, female, late 20's, stylish, made-up, fashionably put together, pretty.

VAL, female, late teens, tomboyish, overly enthusiastic if not hyper.

Premiered in New York City by Artistic New Directions, co-artistic directors Janice L. Goldberg and Kristine Niven, directed by Troy Miller, featuring Leigh Dunham, Lue McWilliams, and Bridget Ori.

SETTING: Midnight, a dog walking park in a suburban neighborhood. Spring.

AT RISE: PRECIOUS stands alone in the moonlight, holding an empty dog leash. Off stage, out front, we hear a dog greet another dog, barking back and forth. She tenses and tries to get her dog's attention to leave.

PRECIOUS: Precious, come on, girl, we're going. Come away from her. Precious, now!

(SAMANTHA enters carrying an empty dog leash. She's too fashionably dressed for dog walking. As their eyes meet, there's a tense moment.)

SAMANTHA: *(Indicating the dogs out front)* Sam misses Precious. A great deal. Hi. So do I. Isn't it...to see how much they. Missing each other. No?

PRECIOUS: Apparently.

SAMANTHA: We've been...for weeks now. And when I hear I've just missed you, I try a little earlier. Then earlier and earlier. It's...it's—

PRECIOUS: So early, it's late. Too late. Precious, come on, girl, we're leaving.

SAMANTHA: No, please, why punish *them*?

PRECIOUS: If you have something to say then by all means... *(Waits for a response but doesn't get one.)* Didn't think so. Well, don't blame me.

SAMANTHA: No, clearly, you blame me. It's not too late. I mean, yes, it's late but...not us. I've...I thought it best to give you space.

PRECIOUS: Another gift? You and your gifts.

SAMANTHA: Please stop dodging us. You said yourself, "dogs need a consistent schedule."

PRECIOUS: If you're confused about "it's over," look it up.

SAMANTHA: I never said that.

PRECIOUS: You took your things and left. That's "it's over." *(Waits for a response but doesn't get one.)* Very well, Precious and I will find another park.

SAMANTHA: No, course not, how does that...I'm trying to...and you're...if you would only...why can't you let me, you know?

PRECIOUS: I'm not hearing one complete sentence.

SAMANTHA: I've been...finding the...to...damn it! Apologize. There, I said it. Satisfied?

PRECIOUS: You named it, you didn't do it.

SAMANTHA: I have many times.

PRECIOUS: No, you haven't; it's never been said once.

SAMANTHA: Yes, with my gifts. I...you've read my—

PRECIOUS: Your gifts remain on the front porch until I give them away.

SAMANTHA: But the notes. I've been...inside, writing long notes full of...explaining. Admitting.

PRECIOUS: Some things aren't for writing.

SAMANTHA: You've been giving away my gifts? *(A coyote howls to the moon.)*

PRECIOUS: *(Off to her dog)* That's right, Precious, don't hold back! Let it out and move on!

SAMANTHA: That's a coyote, not Precious. *(Two dogs start to howl in response.)* That's Precious. And Sam. Like sisters. Family. Apologizing and forgiving.

PRECIOUS: Warning is more like it. Warning the coyote to stay away. Because there are boundaries. But coyotes can be very stubborn. You sure you're allowed out this late? If I were a newlywed, I'd be all cuddled up and cozy.

SAMANTHA: Well, he's snoring away; clueless I'm not even there.

PRECIOUS: You've made your bed, so guess what?

SAMANTHA: Please don't.

PRECIOUS: And I'm so glad we had this lovely moment of closure. Anything else you wanna add before we...? What a sight you are. That leash is a little much, isn't it? Is that bedazzled or Cartier? And are those sensible shoes for walking a dog? French manicure, designer clothes, wow, that's a ring.

SAMANTHA: You make me sound so shallow.

PRECIOUS: Whatever you want to call it. I'd say you're happy. So happy, have you noticed you're putting on a little weight? Even *I* couldn't get you to do that.

SAMANTHA: *(Self-conscious, closing her jacket)* Well...I...maybe I'm slow on the...there's still room for any influence you may have to offer.

PRECIOUS: Nothing. That's what you get now. Everything and nothing.

SAMANTHA: After all you've done for me, let me...I could be...has anyone done yard work since I'm gone? Fixed the back door? Helped you with...whatever. Here...we could...for starters. *(Samantha offers her a $100 bill.)*

PRECIOUS: You're walking the dog with that? Let me guess, you've got so much now, you use it to pick up after Sam?

SAMANTHA: Take it. *(Precious turns away.)* If it weren't for you, I wouldn't know Eva Cassidy; I can't imagine my life without her music. And the Sundance Channel. Bubble tea. Bill Maher. And Ted Talks. I wouldn't be me without you. Please, take it, I'm still...if nothing else, family. No?

PRECIOUS: Were. You ran away. I don't do ex's.

SAMANTHA: Of course you do; it's who we are.

PRECIOUS: It's not funny.

SAMANTHA: I don't know which is funnier. A lesbian who's not family with her ex's, or a lipstick lesbian who no longer wears lipstick.

PRECIOUS: Clearly, we're very different people. At least I can't be bought. Not like you.

SAMANTHA: I never said we were gonna...we had a beautiful...

PRECIOUS: Phase? Please tell me I wasn't a phase. If I had known—

SAMANTHA: And I always wanted...I shared that. My attraction for...having a man on my arm.

PRECIOUS: One who can afford you.

SAMANTHA: Stan can be very generous. To you, too. It could be our little secret. *(In the background, a coyote howls again.)*

PRECIOUS: No coyotes allowed. *(Off to her dog)* Precious, come on, I've had it. As much as I can stand. *(The sound of a third dog joins in with the others, barking.)* What is that? Is it friendly?

SAMANTHA: Looks like a big beagle or something.

PRECIOUS: Whose? Do you know it?

VAL: *(She enters carrying an empty dog leash. She's in her late teens, tomboyish, and hyper. She yells to her dog out front.)* Say "Hey there lovely ladies." No, not that way! Why do you always go right for the ass? MacGregor, wait for permission. *(To the women)* Those yours? MacGregor's a little too eager to say the least. Oh, did I interrupt? I'd say I did. MacGregor, calm the fuck down, you're not a Scottish Terrier! So hyper, those Scots. The kind you want to drop kick. But never would of course. 'Cuz clearly MacGregor's not a Scottish Terrier. Despite his name. Yeah, duh, right? I'm sensing some...a lover's quarrel maybe? Sorry to smile. Not smile as in funny-sneer-I'm-better-than-you, but smile as in...okay, lost it. Yep. Gone. *(To Samantha)* What's that pretty smell, is that you?

SAMANTHA: If you don't mind, we were quietly enjoying the moon.

VAL: Is this a club? Can I join? Is there an initiation?

SAMANTHA: Quietly being the operative word.

VAL: "Operative." Cool. Okay, ignore me; I won't make a sound. Zip. Just quietly admiring two lovely ladies enjoying the moon. I'm Val by the way. Really Valerie, but my granny, oh, shit, sorry. Short-term memory problem. Okay, zip-zip.

PRECIOUS: You're MacGregor, not Val. Otherwise, there're too many names to remember. Makes it less complicated. I'm Precious. Believe it or not.

VAL: *(To Samantha and indicating her dog)* And you must be...don't tell me, something really girlie.

SAMANTHA: Sam.

PRECIOUS: Samantha. After Samantha Stevens.

SAMANTHA: Another cultural treasure you introduced me to.

PRECIOUS: And then you wiggled your nose and disappeared.

SAMANTHA: Maybe I'm more like Serena. Unpredictable.

VAL: Okay, totally lost.

PRECIOUS: It's complicated. *She's* complicated.

SAMANTHA: Tell it to the moon.

PRECIOUS: Maybe I have. Maybe I do.

VAL: I do, too! *(Val howls to the moon with all her spirit.)* Why does that feel so good? Let's do it all together.

SAMANTHA: My oh my, look at the time.

VAL: Or maybe not. Would've been fun. It was for me anyway. But not for you two sticks in the mud.

PRECIOUS: Sticks in the mud? You hear?

SAMANTHA: Don't blame me.

PRECIOUS: I do blame you.

SAMANTHA: I'm the one who's been trying to...and you're not letting me.

PRECIOUS: Why should I? So you can walk out whenever you please?

SAMANTHA: And I don't appreciate you giving away the gifts. You needed that stuff. A toaster, a blender, a proper tool box—

PRECIOUS: All the wedding gifts we never got. What do you know about my needs?

SAMANTHA: You want to end up alone like the moon? Keep it up.

PRECIOUS: The moon understands. Which is more than I can say for you.

VAL: This sure is a lot of tension for bitch-on-bitch playtime.

SAMANTHA: You did not. She did not.

PRECIOUS: She did, and she's right. Two fuddy-duddies, that's what we've become.

VAL: Need a hand? If you're stuck in the mud?

PRECIOUS: Yes, precisely, MacGregor, quick, free us, show us the way.

VAL: On the count of three. *(Val howls to the moon and stops when she realizes she's doing it alone.)*

PRECIOUS: You said on the count of three.

SAMANTHA: Don't encourage her.

PRECIOUS: *(Not sexually speaking)* Why not? She is one fresh drink of water at a time when we are extremely parched.

VAL: *(Searching her pockets)* Oh, shoot, that reminds me. Where did I...? Not again. If I get off schedule, my whole system gets way too enthusiastic and I get on people's nerves. Can you imagine? Damn, I must have...I gotta go. Tomorrow then? Same time, same place?

PRECIOUS: I'm afraid my schedule is a little uncertain.

VAL: I thought we...that we...I always misread things. My fault.

PRECIOUS: But if you're interested, there's a "Bewitched" marathon on this Saturday. I'm at Franklin and Bonnywood.

VAL: The yard that doesn't get mowed?

PRECIOUS: Good, so you know it.

VAL: First thing in the morning? Can MacGregor come? Is it a sleepover? What should I bring?

PRECIOUS: Noon is perfect, MacGregor is welcomed, bring the pills.

VAL: This is...yeah, great. 'Cause I'm never...people don't get me; I'm very misunderstood.

SAMANTHA: And I'm very replaced.

VAL: Hey, maybe if you two could admit what you really mean to each other. Just a thought. My granny always says—*said*, she's dead—you can't pick your nose but you can pick your...no wait, you can pick your nose but you can't pick your...something about family and friends, it's really lovely. Sort of. Shoot, I always mess it up. Oh, the pills! Bye. *(Val kisses Precious on the cheek and runs off.)* Come on, MacGregor. That a girl, yes, we both made friends!

PRECIOUS: Sweet kid. Sent by the moon. Yes. Well, I guess I'm leaving now, too. Unless you have...anything at all?

SAMANTHA: I'm...with all my heart, I...I never meant to...it was the last thing I wanted. To hurt you. But Stan, he...and we...I'm... *(She opens her jacket and indicates her small pregnant belly.)* I didn't know how to tell you. You're very...and I...please believe me, I miss you, I want you in my life. As family. I apologize. If you can forgive me. Just...I hope. *(Off to her dog)* Sam, honey? Guess it's time to go.

PRECIOUS: Join us. Why not? Saturday.

SAMANTHA: For the marathon? I won't be in the way? *(In the background, Val howls to the moon.)*

PRECIOUS: MacGregor's right. We should do it. At the top of our lungs. What do you think?

SAMANTHA: To the moon? Isn't it a bit...?

PRECIOUS: It's what we need. She's right. Will you?

SAMANTHA: Because the moon understands?

PRECIOUS: On the count of three. If you believe in us.

SAMANTHA: For no more stubbornness. And pointless feuds.

PRECIOUS: For never being alone. For extended family.

SAMANTHA: One...

PRECIOUS: Two...

PRECIOUS & SAMANTHA: Three! *(They howl to the moon with all their might, good and long. They take hands.)*

END OF PLAY

(As a reminder, a reduced royalty rate is available, either for individual plays or for a package of six to eight plays. For performance licensing rights, please contact the playwright at www.gregoryfletcher.com)

The Nine-Month Fix
a short play
a drama

by Gregory Fletcher

CAST OF CHARACTERS:

LOU, male, 39 years old, high school educated, formerly a
powerful man, in recovery.

STEPH, female, 22 years old, nine months pregnant, heading to
law school, powerful.

TIME: Early morning, mid-June.

PLACE: Baltimore, an older middle class kitchen with a fresh coat
of paint.

SETTING: At a breakfast table set for two. Much attention has
gone into the preparation.

AT RISE: LOU carries two plates of food to the table.

　　　LOU: *(Calling off)* When you're ready! *(He pours two cups of
coffee.)* It's hot! *(He gets the bread from the toaster and adds them
to the plates.)* Any day now! *(He adjusts a plate so it's just right.
STEPH enters, nine months pregnant, and holds a rolled-up
morning newspaper with disgust.)*

　　　STEPH: Peggy!

　　　LOU: *(Regarding the newspaper)* In the bushes again?

　　　STEPH: Peggy!

　　　LOU: Down at the curb? She's still new at the job, remember.
Her throw *does* need work. I'll speak with her.

STEPH: You'll do no such thing.

LOU: And don't forget, she's still grieving.

STEPH: Big boo-hoo, her and her reckless husband—like you—driving them off a cliff.

LOU: Are you making light of it? He died. It was tragic.

STEPH: That he didn't have life insurance? That now she has to work three jobs, one being a paper route? You're right. Poor thing.

LOU: In your condition, you shouldn't be getting the paper anyway. You need to watch it.

STEPH: Oh, I have been. Nothing you do gets past me. So I thought.

LOU: I'll get the paper for now on. It'll be waiting here for you. *(He pulls out her chair, and she sits with difficulty. The phone rings, and Lou answers it.)* Hello? ... She's right here. Anxious to speak to you, I'm sure. *(Lou brings the phone to Steph.)*

STEPH: Hello? *(She melts.)* Hi, Mommy. How's life on the ocean? ... As nice as Fiji? ... Keep those postcards coming for the scrapbook. I'm calling it, "A Lifetime of Vacations, Taken All At Once." Right? ... Your charges are fine. ... Seriously, we didn't expect you to stay on the boat for six months. Of course you're gonna take tours and excursions. Live it up. Hey, remember how you thought six months was too long to be away? Still feel that way? *(Laughs)* Well, you deserve it. Another week, your boat docks, you'll be home, and life will begin anew. ... No, I'll most likely be setting up in New York, but Lou will be there with bells on. Maybe literally if he doesn't watch it. ... I promise to come home a.s.a.p. *(Looks to Lou)* Yeah, Lou, he's fine, slowly but surely. *(The baby kicks; she rubs her belly.)* He'll be a good daddy if it kills me. Listen. I'm. I've. *(Changes her mind.)* Someone's at the door; I'll call you back soon. ... In a few. ... I don't know.

Minutes. In a few. ... Mom, in a friggin' few! ... Okay, love you, too. *(Steph hangs up the phone and tries to hold it together.)*

LOU: "Someone's at the door?" *(No response)* Should I get it?

STEPH: I almost told her. After all we've been through. You actually had me considering keeping the baby. But one baby is enough. So here's what we do, *baby*. Fixing another problem. You will never make contact with her again.

LOU: Your mother?

STEPH: *(She pulls out a hidden frilly note with disgust from inside the newspaper.)* Peggy! And her special deliveries. And cheap perfume. And hiding it in the Sports section of all places. How long has it been? Are we starting over after six friggin' months?

LOU: No. I don't know what she's doing.

STEPH: Oh, I do. It's obvious when you read it. The love note. Made me wanna throw up. Just when I thought we were making progress. *(Steph indicates a woman's frilly apron.)* Forgetting something? Or would you like to be back to riding my little girl bike to work again?

LOU: *(Reluctantly, putting on the apron.)* It's nothing with Peggy. Just so you know.

STEPH: It's over with Peggy. Just so *you* know. Damn it! I've been suspicious ever since you put money in her cup. Months ago at the mall. Another kick in the stomach, I don't need.

LOU: It's nothing, lots of people were putting money in her cup.

STEPH: Ringing her bell, making a racket.

LOU: Christmas charity.

STEPH: And you gave on the way in, and on the way out. And that look between you two. It was the only time she stopped ringing her friggin' bell. Thank God I ran into *him* later that spring.

I asked him what he thought. And, guess what, he had been suspicious all along, too.

LOU: He who?

STEPH: What's his name, her dead husband, the lousy driver. Did you know he's got quite the temper? Excuse me. Had. Sorry. He wanted to pay you a little visit, but I promised to handle you myself. And *he* promised to handle Peggy. "To get to the bottom of it." And, boy, did he ever.

LOU: My God. His car off that cliff.

STEPH: Yeah, I don't think that's what he had in mind.

LOU: You...that was you?

STEPH: Me? It was you. You and Peggy!

LOU: So it wasn't an accident. Steph, for God's sake, do you know what you've done?

STEPH: Me? Seriously? You have the nerve to...me?! *(She shoves the table, feels pain in her belly, calms herself.)*

LOU: I'm sorry. I...you're not to blame.

STEPH: So what's it gonna be? It's up to you, believe it or not.

LOU: My family is here. My commitment is here. My public pledge and holy sacrament, it's all here.

STEPH: And your love?

LOU: Give me that thing. *(Lou tears Peggy's note into pieces. Steph indicates for him to sit. He does so and they take hands and bow their heads.)*

STEPH & LOU: God is great, God is good, let us thank Him for this food.

LOU: Amen.

STEPH: And give us the strength, dear Lord, to bring this ordeal to a close. Nourish our bodies and let us see the light this new day. Amen.

LOU: Our newly enlightened selves. To renewed commitments and beginnings. Amen.

STEPH: "Newly enlightened? Renewed commitments?" You better not be playing me. Okay. Here's how we solve this one. Get the pen and pad. *(He does so, and Steph writes.)* Dial her number.

LOU: Your mother?

STEPH: Peggy's! *(Lou reluctantly dials the phone number.)* Read this like you mean it. And don't change a word.

LOU: It'll go right to voicemail.

STEPH: Good. She can play it over and over. Did it beep?

LOU: It's still the greeting.

STEPH: "Hi, this is Peggy, I date married men no more." Here. *(She slides the pad to him.)*

LOU: *(Into the phone, reading)* "I never want to see you again. Or read your hidden stupid notes. If you ever contact me again, I'll tell Father Dewey about us. And I'll tell the cops the car accident was no accident. You hear me? It's over."

STEPH: And cancel the paper.

LOU: "And cancel the paper."

STEPH: There is no more *Baltimore Sun* for me.

LOU: "There is no more *Baltimore Sun* for me."

STEPH: Hang up. *(Lou hangs up and recovers.)* You need to know that if anything starts up again between you two, I will make a very public scene with accusations that will follow you the rest of your life. Got it?

LOU: Yeah. Loud and clear.

STEPH: I know it feels like this whole ordeal has been all about you, but actually it's been about my mother. All for Mom. Which is why I'm keeping it simple.

LOU: Sending your mother on a six-month world cruise has been far from simple. Would you like to see the bank statement?

STEPH: Too bad. Could've been worse. Still could. What you don't get is this: it's my body, my baby, *I* get the final say.

LOU: Abandoning my flesh and blood at a hospital is not something I can live with. You said you'd figure it out. You said my mind was clear and sound. That I was a new man. I've more than proven myself. Steph, we gotta keep this baby.

STEPH: We? I'm starting law school in the fall, and this unwanted baby isn't coming with me. Forget it, as if this whole thing's not creepy enough.

LOU: I've gone with everything you said for six months now. I've taken responsibility for my actions.

STEPH: Oh, you have? Then why haven't you apologized? You forgot that, too? *(No response)* You wanna keep this baby or not?

LOU: Yes. Absolutely.

STEPH: Then friggin' apologize.

LOU: Okay. You're right. I'm sorry.

STEPH: That's all I get?

LOU: What I put you through. The drunkin' nights and all.

STEPH: Say the words. What you did.

LOU: For drinking so much, you had to come find me. In that awful bar. So late. Stumbling to the car, parked in the alleyway. Passing the two guys sitting on the hood of their car.

STEPH: That's more than you've ever said before. Them offering to help? Taking you by the arms? Throwing you against the wall?

LOU: *(Shrugs)* I'm sorry for not being able to defend you.

STEPH: Go on.

LOU: For not preventing their...what they did to you. For not being able to ID them. For not being able to strangle them with my bare hands.

STEPH: Name it. *(Lou cannot.)* Are you denying it happened? *(Indicating her belly.)* Isn't this proof enough?

LOU: For not protecting my only daughter. While they...raped you. I'm sorry. I promise you, I will never let you down again. You or the baby. You'll see.

STEPH: Anybody else?

LOU: Yeah, sure, let's get her on the phone. Tell her about the baby. How I failed you. How I'll make it up to you. Please.

STEPH: *(Getting a possible idea.)* Didn't Mom used to talk about adopting? She did, right?

LOU: Since the hysterectomy, yeah.

STEPH: *(Dials a phone number)* What about telling her, after years of being on a waiting list, you've finally made it to the top.

LOU: *(Into the phone, after a connection, with too much enthusiasm.)* Margie? Our name is up. It's been years since I put our names on the list; I completely forgot. But they just called.

STEPH: That was them at the door.

LOU: And stopped by. That was them at the door. Doing a surprise meet and greet. And we passed, can you believe it? ... We're adopting a baby! ... Because I didn't wanna get your hopes up if it didn't happen. Not after all I've put you through. Margie, I'm sorry for being such a prick. For not making you feel special these last years. But no more. I've got my head on straight. Had some help during your time away. Steph saw to that. I haven't had a drink in almost six months. I go to meetings now. I help out around the house. I can work the washing machine, the dishwasher, I help with the cooking. I painted the house from top to bottom, inside and out. ... Hold on. *(Lou gives the phone to Steph.)*

STEPH: Yes? ... No, he's completely sober. ... I promise you, he's not smoking "the crack." Mom, it's all true, no joke. The adoption papers are being drawn up, all approved, baby due any day now. ... I know, right? Hey, we'll meet your boat with baby in tow. ... Yes, I'll be there. And miss your face when Dad hands you the baby? ... Rest while you can. Talk soon.

LOU: *(Yelling toward the phone.)* I love you, Margie! Always have! Always will! *(Steph hangs up.)* She sounded so happy.

STEPH: *(Taking off Lou's girlie apron.)* It's done.

LOU: Is it? *(Steph agrees.)* I promise to treat your mother like a queen.

STEPH: Your wife. As she deserves.

LOU: Yes, my wife. As she deserves. And the baby, too.

STEPH: *(Her water breaks and hits the floor.)* What the—

LOU: Stephy?

STEPH: Daddy?

LOU: I'll get your bag. *(Lou rushes off.)*

STEPH: *(She speed dials on her cell-phone.)* It's time; I'm going in. ... Is the ID ready? ... Thank God. I won't have time to come get it; my water just broke. Can you meet me at the turn in? ... No, nothing but a change of clothes. *(Takes her wallet from her bag and leaves it in a drawer.)* Hey. Wondering if you know anyone who can do adoption papers? ... A week or so. ... Patty, you are one gifted woman. ... Whatever the price, it'll be worth it. See ya in a few. *(Steph disconnects the call, and Lou returns with a small overnight bag.)* Do not come in with me, or visit, or call. You'll see me when I'm back here with the baby.

LOU: Look at you. You pulled it off. Just like you said you would. Turned things around 180 degrees. You're something else, you know it?

STEPH: *(Feels pain and breathes through it.)* Ah! Well. Okay. Here's to new beginnings. You ready? *(Lou agrees, and they exit.)*

END OF PLAY

(As a reminder, a reduced royalty rate is available, either for individual plays or for a package of six to eight plays. For performance licensing rights, please contact the playwright at www.gregoryfletcher.com)

Not Tonight
a short play
a drama

by Gregory Fletcher

CAST OF CHARACTERS:

BOBBI, female, in her late 40's.

BILL, male, in his mid 20's.

ROSS, male, in his late 40's.

TIME: 2013.

AT RISE: In darkness, gunfire battles, an aggressive stand off. A plane flies by and a bomb explodes nearby. As a doorbell chimes, lights up on a living room area and front door of a middle class home. BILL sits up from the couch, gasping. Nearby, turning from the peephole at the front door, BOBBI gasps at the same time. Bill calms his panic attack; Bobbi is unable to calm hers. She's dressed in a bathrobe and slippers. A clock chimes six times.

BOBBI: *(Whispering)* I should've known they'd try this early. Every other time they've shown up, I've dodged them.

BILL: You're not dressed for company, and I sure as hell don't want any.

BOBBI: You can't ignore them. Even if they leave, they just come back again and again. Until they get you.

BILL: Who? Nobody's getting anybody. *(He takes off his t-shirt and wipes the sweat from his face. He wears military tags around his neck.)* Why are you dressed for bed already? *(He grabs a clean t-shirt from a nearby laundry basket of clothes and puts it on.)* Come sit down.

BOBBI: I was always sure they'd get me when opening the garage door. Every time it goes up, I'm on pins and needles to see if two pairs of black shiny dress shoes are waiting. And then two creased pairs of slacks. Jackets. Holding their hat like so. Standing there with their solemn faces. But they've never come this early before.

BILL: Take a breath.

BOBBI: They never had any luck getting me as I pulled in. When I see their car out front, I just keep driving like I don't even live here. I don't care how much gas it takes; I'll drive around for hours, if need be.

BILL: When was this?

BOBBI: Or when they come right after dinnertime when I'm doing the dishes. I slip right out the backdoor and cut through the Lanty's yard.

BILL: Come away from the door; there's no one there.

BOBBI: *(The doorbell chimes again, and she gestures for him to keep quiet.)* You sit down and shut up.

BILL: That's nice.

BOBBI: There's nothing nice about it. You talk to them, and it's a done deal. I want that Chaplain and the other good for nothing officer off my porch this minute. I won't hear a word. Not a word. *(The doorbell chimes again, and she almost collapses.)* Oh, my good God, not Billy. Please. Not my sweet Billy. *(Bill stands and goes for the door.)* No, don't! This is no way to start the day! I won't hear it! *(Bill opens the door and finds ROSS, holding a large pizza box. Bill takes the pizza box, leaves it on the coffee table, and exits. Bobbi moves to Ross in the doorway and looks past him to the street.)*

ROSS: Hey, Bobbi. Good *evening.*

BOBBI: *(Relieved)* Guess so.

ROSS: I can't vouch for "piping hot." I rang a few times.

BOBBI: All paid for?

ROSS: No worries.

BOBBI: *(She moves to the drawer of a side table and pulls two bills from a man's wallet and gives it to him.)* No worries. No worries. I'm sorry it can't be more.

ROSS: Hey—

BOBBI: Hey, yourself. *(She closes the door and locks it. Bill enters with a roll of paper towels and two beers.)*

BILL: I didn't know what you wanted to drink.

BOBBI: When you're expecting somebody, wait by the door and answer it yourself!

BILL: *(Opening the box and taking out a slice.)* This wasn't my idea. I didn't order it.

BOBBI: Oh, look, your favorite. Extra mushrooms. How you torment me! *(She exits. Bill picks off the mushrooms from his slice and leaves them in the box. After a bite, he moves to the front door, opens it, and returns to the couch.)*

BILL: Not hungry?

ROSS: Sometimes, it's best to wait. *(Bill hands him the second bottle of beer.)* So. You saw. Good.

BILL: Seriously? In the hour you've been gone? Yeah, I was too busy to notice. I got a job, recruited for a hockey team, doctor lowered my meds, said I'll be like normal any day now.

ROSS: I meant your mother. Was hoping her being alone with you might...reverse things a little. Since you're finally home. Well, at least now you see what I'm saying.

BILL: Not really.

ROSS: She thought I was the pizza guy.

BILL: No, she didn't.

ROSS: She tipped me.

BILL: I thought you said she had no money. Wasn't that a rule? Don't give her any money or car keys? *(Ross holds up the two bills, and Bill checks his wallet in the side table.)* I'm missing forty bucks.

ROSS: A very generous tip. *(Offering him the bills.)* I'd keep it on you at all times, if I were you.

BILL: Keep it.

ROSS: When you get a job.

BILL: I start tomorrow.

ROSS: When you *keep* a job.

BILL: Oh give me a friggin' break; it was my first day and working at a bowling alley wasn't the smartest idea with all that noise. Just keep it. In food alone, I'm costing you plenty.

ROSS: That's what parents do; we feed our kids. And house them when needed.

BILL: I haven't been a burden since high school and now I'm back to where I started.

ROSS: Considering you're just back from...give yourself a break. And do me a favor, will ya? Don't think of this job, whatever it is, as your new life career. Just let it get you back up on your feet, that's all. *(Ross reluctantly pockets the money.)*

BILL: And next time, easy on the mushrooms. *(They eat. Ross takes the discarded mushrooms and adds them to his slice.)* Mom used to be so cheap with tipping.

ROSS: She eats broccoli now. And cauliflower. All vegetables but one. Green beans.

BILL: That was the only one she ever ate.

ROSS: Only if it were French cut and canned. *(After a moment)* Hey, feel like clearing out your old room tonight?

BILL: What am I supposed to do with all the unopened merchandise? It's like a department store in there.

ROSS: How about selling it on eBay? You know how to do that?

BILL: Won't Mom just buy more?

ROSS: She no longer has a credit card, so her shopping frenzies are done. Thank God. As I was saying earlier, she—

BILL: As you were *exaggerating* earlier, and always have. How many miles of snow did you walk to school in?

ROSS: One point two five.

BILL: One point two five? It's been between three and seven my entire life; now, it's one point two five?

ROSS: Well, I'm more of a realist these days.

BILL: A realist and a vegetarian.

ROSS: I still eat meat. Just not in the house. It can sometimes...turn things. Send her. I don't know.

BILL: Exactly, you don't know. She's too cooped up. She needs some fresh air. Some exercise.

ROSS: She doesn't recognize us.

BILL: Look at me; I've changed a bit. She's just...I think she thinks that I've been...that there were two officers coming to report that I was...has anybody come by?

ROSS: They don't come to the house when you're coming home.

BILL: To say that I was shot. Injured.

ROSS: That was a telephone call. And by the way, she won't answer the phone either. Look, this isn't my opinion, okay? Your mother's getting...every month, it's worse.

BILL: For how long?

ROSS: I started noticing things during your first tour.

BILL: My first? That's a long time ago.

ROSS: It's been slow moving.

BILL: So see a specialist. Get a second opinion. I could bring her in with me on Thursday. My doctor could at least make a recommendation.

ROSS: Billy, we're way past that.

BILL: Then why haven't you mentioned it?

ROSS: I'm telling you now.

BILL: You were waiting to see if I came home. *(No response)* Yeah. It would've been easier if I came home in a box.

ROSS: Actually, I could use your help.

BILL: From me? That's funny. If you haven't noticed, I've got my own problems. *(Regrets his response.)* Sorry.

BOBBI: *(Off-stage)* Hey, bath man. Baaath Maaan.

ROSS: That would be me.

BILL: So where do you take her when you're at work?

ROSS: She has a...what d'ya call it...daycare that I drop her at.

BILL: She's doing crafts? That's how you're helping her?

ROSS: No, they're medical people. And others like her.

BILL: She talked like she still drives the car.

ROSS: Not in months. Almost a year.

BOBBI: *(She enters wearing an old bathing suit.)* The tub feels solid; it's not going anywhere tonight.

ROSS: Bubbles or no bubbles? Pink or blue?

BOBBI: Blue. *(Ross exits.)* The tub was against me last week. Too many bubbles. But we're all friends again. No grudges. If that's possible. But none of us are on the same team. And that's the thing with teams. You're rooting for one team and trying to bring down the other. And I sure as heck don't wanna end up in the basement. The tub can just open up when it wants. Even when we make nice, one team still wants to see the other fail. Conquered. And before you know it, we're fighting and not knowing why we're fighting. Or worse yet, fighting for lies we think are the truth. Fighting for the team. The team. Why can't we all be on the same team? Winning is no fun when others lose. And losing...well, it's...at some...point, it'll be...yeah. *(Touching Bill's face.)* I forgot how handsome you are. The older you get, the more I see Billy in you. Billy with the sparkle in his eyes. Like after a game with his wind burned face and chill from his rosy cheeks. Exhausted, bruised, but always with that sparkle in his eye. Whether the team won or not. He'd pick me up, straight into the air. I looked forward to it every single game. Pick me up. *(She raises her arms to be lifted.)* Pick me up, Billy, like after the game. Win or lose, I'm up in the air. So glorious. For too brief a moment. Pick me up. Can't you do it anymore? *(Bill squats and wraps his arms around her legs and lifts her straight up. Her arms sway in the air. Ross enters.)* Oh, Billy. Sweet Billy. My Billy. Please, don't go. Why must you go? There won't be any winners. Just losers. We're all being conquered, like it or not. But don't...stupid boy. To volunteer? Don't you see? Can't you see? What am I going to do without you? *(Billy tries hard to hold it together emotionally.)*

ROSS: Your bath is just like you like it.

BILL: *(He slowly sets her down.)* Mom, I'm not going anywhere. I'm home now. It's me, Billy. I'm gonna help you the best I can, okay? *(Bobbie slaps him across the face and exits.)*

ROSS: You okay? Sometimes it turns so fast, I don't see it coming.

BILL: I'm not qualified.

ROSS: You're a soldier, of course you are. I should watch her.

BILL: But, Dad. What can I...? I'm not.... We gotta to do something. Who can we call?

BOBBI: *(Off-stage)* No one is to ring that bell tonight. Promise me. No ringing bells of any kind. Somebody promise me. No ringing bells. *(Ross looks to Bill who nods and understands now. Ross is relieved. Both step together to connect physically, maybe embrace, but it's a failed attempt. Ross looks off to Bobbi, knowing he should be there. Bill gestures for him to go. Ross agrees and exits, leaving Bill alone.)*

END OF PLAY

(As a reminder, a reduced royalty rate is available, either for individual plays or for a package of six to eight plays. For performance licensing rights, please contact the playwright at www.gregoryfletcher.com)

Roast Beef and the Rare Kiss
a short play
a romantic comedy

by Gregory Fletcher

CAST OF CHARACTERS:

ALAN, male, mid-to-late 20's.

PAULA, female, mid-to-late 20's.

DEE, female, mid-to-late 20's.

TIM, male, mid-to-late 20's.

Premiered at Boston Theatre Marathon, artistic director Kate
Snodgrass, directed by Patricia Riggin, featuring Christopher
Barnard, Stephanie Marquis, Sarah Nowalk, and Li Trew.
Produced in New York City by the Emerging Artists Theatre,
artistic director Paul Adams, directed by Troy Miller, featuring
Patrick Arnheim, Matt Boethin, Lavette Gleis, and Danae Hanson.
Later, in New York City by Artistic New Directions, co-artistic
directors Janice L. Goldberg and Kristine Niven, directed by Troy
Miller, featuring Nicholas Cocchetto, Leigh Dunham, David
Marshall, Bridget Ori.

Finalist for the National Ten-Minute Play Contest and Heideman
Award at the Actors' Theatre of Louisville, and nominee for
Outstanding Original Short Script for the New York IT Awards
(celebrating Off-Off-Broadway).

SETTING: A comfy sofa big enough for four adults, with two used red wine glasses and dessert plates on a coffee table. There's also an empty wine bottle and a DVD remote control.

AT RISE: ALAN and PAULA are sitting on the sofa and kissing. The kiss is tender, lovely, and sexy, and continues for a good long time.

ALAN: *(Not finding the words.)* Wow.

PAULA: Yeah. My stomach is shaking.

ALAN: Look at the hair on my arm.

PAULA: Like I'm back in—

ALAN: High school. Me, too.

PAULA: Yes. So unexpected. Surprising.

ALAN: And yet...

PAULA: So...

ALAN: Lovely?

PAULA: Exactly. Your lips.

ALAN: My lips?

PAULA: I've been wanting to—

ALAN: Me, too.

PAULA: Seriously? Us?

ALAN: Yes, I've been...

PAULA: Since when? Why didn't you?

ALAN: I've even dreamt about it.

PAULA: With me? Get out.

ALAN: And we were naked, too.

PAULA: Really? Shut up. How naked?

ALAN: Well, we were taking a bath.

PAULA: That sounds very naked.

ALAN: Yep. Naked.

PAULA: Any bubbles?

ALAN: And candles and classical music, it was amazing. A claw foot bathtub.

PAULA: Oh, I love those. So big. So deep.

ALAN: Yeah, so big, so deep, so porno sounding.

PAULA: It was me; my description of a claw foot bathtub oddly turned...tell me more.

ALAN: Well, not much else really. I almost drowned. Foot massage always makes me melt. And we were doing each other. Foot massage. And we were...we were both melting.

PAULA: Sounds...intriguing. Yes.

ALAN: Yes, it does.

(DEE enters from the kitchen and picks up the remaining two dessert plates and wine bottle.)

DEE: Yes what does?

PAULA: Oh my God, how funny!

ALAN: Where-where-where you been? What-what-what you doing?

DEE: Are you stuttering?

ALAN: I always...uh...stutter after a good meal. You never no-no-noticed? See?

DEE: We can handle a triple batch, right?

PAULA: As always.

DEE: Parmesan mixed in?

ALAN: Just like I like it.

PAULA: But not too much salt. Tim's the same.

DEE: He's hiding the salt as we speak. Isn't this the perfect end to a perfect evening? *(Dee kisses Alan on the cheek and exits.)*

ALAN: Yeah. Perfect.

PAULA: What were we thinking?

ALAN: It's my fault.

PAULA: It was me; I take full—

ALAN: Right in the next room, what the—

PAULA: I know, right? I mean—

ALAN: Awful. But thank God she didn't—

PAULA: No, don't even go there. We...we're—

ALAN: Absolutely. Totally safe. Lucky us.

PAULA: Yes. Whew.

ALAN: Alright. Well.

PAULA: But I am glad we...

ALAN: Oh, definitely, yes. But why chance it?

PAULA: Oh, you don't have to tell me. *(Indicating the kitchen.)* Best friends. To give that up?

ALAN: And this would certainly—

PAULA: In a heartbeat. Gone.

ALAN: Destroyed.

PAULA: And friendships like ours—

ALAN: Once in a lifetime.

PAULA: If you're lucky.

ALAN: Exactly.

(TIM enters from the kitchen and picks up the remaining wine glasses.)

TIM: That's it for the wine.

ALAN: Should I run out? I can run out. Yeah, I'll run out. Good idea, I'm gonna run out.

TIM: No need. We can move on to the hard stuff. Any objections? *(Noticing Paula turning away from him.)* Did I interrupt?

PAULA: Don't be silly. Waiting on you.

TIM: All cued up?

ALAN: Wish you two would hurry.

TIM: Back in a flash.

PAULA: You're the best, Timmy.

TIM: And you're the only person in the entire world who gets to call me Timmy. *(Tim kisses Paula, then notices Alan.)* You okay?

ALAN: Sure.

PAULA: Why wouldn't he be?

ALAN: Just craving the umm-umm-umm—

TIM: Popcorn? Wow, you're in rare form. Any minute now. *(Tim exits.)*

ALAN: It never happened. No jokes, no hints.

PAULA: No double entendres, no code words.

ALAN: There's always truth in a tease; it gets me in trouble all the time.

PAULA: Deal. Starting now. Change the subject. Dee's an excellent cook.

ALAN: Yes, her roast beef is...I tell everyone, I always have... never ever in my life...absolutely the...it's so...you know?

PAULA: I do. So perfect and...and—

ALAN: Rare?

PAULA: Yes, it was.

ALAN: Hmmm. Delicious.

PAULA: And lovely.

ALAN: Rare and lovely. *(Deliberately changing the subject.)* And Tim was so funny with the—

PAULA: Wasn't that funny? Oh my God, so funny! He is so funny! Funny-funny.

(Dee enters with a big bowl of popcorn, and Tim carries four martinis on a tray.)

DEE: Look who's having all the fun in here.

TIM: Is there a designated driver I should know about before it's too late?

PAULA: I thought it was you.

DEE: If there's too much Parmesan—

TIM: I didn't know; I didn't see any.

DEE: Because I mixed it up.

TIM: I didn't see. Who could see it?

ALAN & PAULA: Too much Parmesan? Impossible.

TIM: Thank you. Thank you both. And in stereo.

DEE: Oh shoot, forgot the napkins.

TIM: I'll get them.

DEE: *(Starting out)* It's okay, you'll never find them.

TIM: What are you implying, I'm stupid? *(Following her out with the popcorn bowl.)* And we should divide this up so there's less reaching.

DEE: What are *you* implying?

TIM: That I want more than my share.

DEE. So it's not too obvious?

TIM: Or I'm speaking for you and just being polite? *(Tim and Dee laugh off-stage.)*

ALAN: They know.

PAULA: Yep, it's over.

ALAN: Did you see the way he was glaring at me?

PAULA: How about her. "Look who's having all the fun in here."

ALAN: We're done for.

PAULA: Completely. Unless...no. Well...unless...

ALAN: We disappeared and lived in another city maybe?

PAULA: Where we could entirely start over?

ALAN: With new friends.

PAULA: New parents.

ALAN: New parents? I like my parents.

PAULA: But they'd never understand. After all we've put them through?

ALAN: You're right. New family altogether. And new memberships.

PAULA: And with kids. Two point five. Little Paula and little Alan.

ALAN: And point five. Why are we...?

PAULA: Are you...?

ALAN: Because I'm not—

PAULA: No, no, things are great.

ALAN: Super great.

PAULA: Seriously.

ALAN: 'Cause it's not like I'm reaching out or unhappy or—

PAULA: *(Indicating the kitchen.)* I am so in love, completely in love, without a doubt.

ALAN: Us, too, incredibly in love. *(Indicating his wedding ring.)* Until death do us part.

PAULA: Not even then. Forever and ever.

ALAN: Absolutely.

PAULA: Good. Yeah.

ALAN: So.

(Dee and Tim return with napkins and two bowls of popcorn.)

TIM: Guess who added salt to her bowl?

DEE: *Sea* salt, it's not the same. Stop trying to get me in trouble.

TIM: Me? I would never.

ALAN: Curtain going up? *(Dee couples up with Paula; Tim couples up with Alan.)*

DEE: Oh, I love the little things in life. *(Paula kisses Dee long and very much in love.)*

TIM: Especially Friday film nights. *(Alan kisses Tim long and very much in love.)*

DEE: We're all so sickeningly sweet, I love it.

PAULA: You two are gonna miss the film.

TIM: I plan to cry good and hard.

DEE: Me, too.

(Dee points the remote, and a romantic film score swells. As everyone settles into the opening moments, Alan and Paula slowly look to one another.)

<u>END OF PLAY</u>

(As a reminder, a reduced royalty rate is available, either for individual plays or for a package of six to eight plays. For performance licensing rights, please contact the playwright at <u>www.gregoryfletcher.com</u>)

Robert Mapplethorpe's Flowers
a short play
a romantic comedy

by Gregory Fletcher

<u>CAST OF CHARACTERS</u>:

GARY, male, 50's.

SCOTT, male, 50's.

Premiered in Boston by SlamBoston/Another Country Productions, artistic director Lyralen Kaye, directed by Joseph Walsh, featuring Chris Clark and Michael Cuddire. Then produced in Provincetown at the Provincetown Fringe Festival, directed by Judith Partelow, featuring Stuard Derrick and Jeff Spencer, which subsequently moved to New York City to the Spotlight On Festival in Greenwich Street Theatre. Also included in Miami at the Lavender Footlights Festival, produced by Creative Arts Enterprises.

Originally published in *Wilde Magazine*.

SETTING: At a dining table in Scott's and Gary's home.

AT RISE: GARY sets a photography book by Robert Mapplethorpe on the table and makes sure everything is just as planned. He exits and returns with SCOTT. Gary pulls out a chair for Scott.

GARY: Page 67.

SCOTT: *(Opening the book to the page.)* "Easter Lilies with Mirror, 1979." *(Looking at the opposite page)* And hel-lo.

GARY: No-no, don't look there. Stay focused. Page 67.

SCOTT: Might be hard...so to speak. Yep, no "might" about it. Lucky dog. Caught at his peak. So proud, so cocky, so—

GARY: You mind? Page 67, "The Easter Lilies."

SCOTT: Yes, and they're proud too. When you're that exquisite, who wouldn't be?

GARY: Tell me what you see.

SCOTT: Five squares in the shape of a cross.

GARY: And?

SCOTT: With Easter Lilies.

GARY: And?

SCOTT: Don't be mad if this doesn't work.

GARY: Scott! I mean...honey. Why would...how could I be mad? Whatever happens, happens. *(Indicates page 67.)*

SCOTT: Yes, so proud, so studly. That unashamed youthful arrogance.

GARY: The Easter Lilies?

SCOTT: How can I not look at him? And admire. And long for. Remember when...never mind.

GARY: It was a moment in time. I guarantee he's not that studly anymore. And certainly not that youthful. For all we know, he could be our age.

SCOTT: As old as that?

GARY: Shut-up. Page 167. "Orchid, 1987."

SCOTT: *(Turning to the page.)* Okay. Yes.

GARY: Yes, what?

SCOTT: Umm...well...what was the question?

GARY: *(Closing the book.)* You're not even trying.

SCOTT: You're the one who banned the porn. And now I can't even look at an art book?

GARY: Because you'll end up getting angry.

SCOTT: I do not.

GARY: Disappointed. Melancholy. You do, too.

SCOTT: Maybe. *(Opening the book to page 167 and concentrating on the flowers.)* Okay, ummm, completely open. Balanced on a stem. Which is slightly leaning toward the left. Like you. Sorry.

GARY: What else?

SCOTT: Where the stem attaches is like...well, like a scrotum. *(Gary gives him a look.)* Well, it is. And the two leaves reaching out on either side are like inviting arms saying come and have me. Come and enjoy me. I am here for you. Take me.

GARY: Nice.

SCOTT: And the big leaf on top standing erect and straight up is like the upper body that will bend down as you come in for a taste. Lying gently on your back, caressing you, whispering, yeah, that's right, go for it, you got me now.

GARY: Hmmm. Very good.

SCOTT: And there's peach fuzz that's almost like body hair, did you notice? There's a slight glisten in the light.

GARY: Yes.

SCOTT: And the texture to the leaves is very much like skin. So alive and inviting. Come. Come. Mapplethorpe's really something else.

GARY: Moving on. Pages 182 and 183.

SCOTT: *(Turning to the pages.)* Oh my good God.

GARY: Yes?

SCOTT: The colors. So vibrant.

GARY: Yes.

SCOTT: Closed with a foreskin of leaves standing perfectly up and guarding...protecting the prized possession.

GARY: *(Naming it)* "Tulip, 1988."

SCOTT: And the other one.

GARY: "Orchid, 1988."

SCOTT: Completely open, as open as one can be before getting there. It's working.

GARY: Yeah?

SCOTT: Like goose bumps shooting up the back of my neck and out the tips of my ears.

GARY: Page 58.

SCOTT: *(Turning the pages)* Oh, Gary, you're so brilliant.

GARY: "Tiger Lily, 1977."

SCOTT: Shit!

GARY: What?

SCOTT: Patti Smith. What the hell? Why is she here?

GARY: Don't look.

SCOTT: I might as well flip to the old broad carrying the huge dildo.

GARY: Page 58, don't look at the portraits.

SCOTT: *(Turning to another wrong page.)* "Marty Going Down On Veronica, 1982!" Didn't need to see that, now did I?

GARY: You can't wander in this book; it's dangerous.

SCOTT: *(Turning pages again.)* Oh, no, the self-portraits!

GARY: I'm not looking. With the whip?

SCOTT: What was he thinking?

GARY: Quick, page 58!

SCOTT: So bi-polar.

GARY: For the love of God, "Tiger Lily," page 58.

SCOTT: I can't find it.

GARY: Alright, skipping. Page 102.

SCOTT: It was working. Was.

GARY: No pressure. No worries.

SCOTT: It was working. Going so well.

GARY: We'll get it back; we've got time. Wait 'til you see "Baby's Breath" and "Orchid and Leaf in White Vase, 1982."

SCOTT: Which page? Speak very clearly, and I'll try to be careful.

GARY: Page 1-0-2. *(Scott opens the book and stares.)* Why aren't you turning? Oh. Him.

SCOTT: "Man in Polyester Suit, 1980."

GARY: You can't just randomly open it up like that. Wait until you see the correct page number first.

SCOTT: What a misleading title, "Man in Polyester Suit." Don't think so. "Man Sticking Out of Polyester Suit" is more like it.

GARY: I should have color copied the pages I wanted.

SCOTT: Immortalized in his youthful glory for eternity. Remember at the Whitney how we watched people's faces as they entered the room seeing it? Has one man ever dropped so many jaws? I've ruined it.

GARY: No, I didn't think it through. I forgot how much room there was for distraction.

SCOTT: *(Turning to another page.)* "Mr. 10 ½!" Now, he's accurately titled. Placed on a countertop like a slab of meat. Remember when I tried it once? It wasn't the same.

GARY: Let's take a break; we can try again later. When you're less...less...

SCOTT: Shallow? That would be a relief.

GARY: Listen, real sexual passion wins over body image and youth any day. *(They consider the thought, then laugh hysterically. Gary pinches himself to stop.)* I mean it. This is not laughing. It's...I'm being...

SCOTT: Of course, I know. Exactly. I'm right with ya.

GARY: These flowers, they're all we need now.

SCOTT: Where were we? Let's continue.

GARY: No, some other time. Wanna take a walk?

SCOTT: No, pages 102 and 103, right? *(Turning a few pages and stops.)* Richard Gere. So angelic, so young.

GARY: Weren't we all at one point? And we move on.

SCOTT: Grudgingly. *(Turning to another page.)* "Arnold Schwarzenegger, 1976." Yep, that's a long time ago.

GARY: Have you seen him lately?

SCOTT: No comment. *(Gary closes the book.)* What're you doing? *(Gary moves the book.)* No, I really want to. *(Gary reaches underneath the table and lifts a vase with a single Calla Lily or any phallic sexy flower.)* Oh, Gary, where did you...? Gorgeous.

GARY: It's not just his photos, is it?

SCOTT: It takes my breath away.

GARY: So...delectable.

SCOTT: Heightened. Erect.

GARY: Engorged. Solid.

SCOTT: Strong.

GARY: Yes.

SCOTT: Yes.

GARY: So arousing.

SCOTT: So uncircumcised and in his full glory.

GARY: Yes. *(Opening the book and showing a photo.)* "The Calla Lily Duo, 1988." It's us.

SCOTT: Us?

GARY: You and me.

SCOTT: Yes?

GARY: Us. Together now so long.

SCOTT: Twenty years.

GARY: How many?

SCOTT: In two years, three months, and a day.

GARY: Alive and well.

SCOTT: And passionate and hungry and everything else we had.

GARY: *Have.*

SCOTT: Yes, I want that. I do.

GARY: Were two words ever so beautiful?

SCOTT: "I do."

GARY: When we let all this other stuff go, 'cause it means nothing. *(Scott nods, agreeing.)* All ours. You and me.

SCOTT: It's...I...I feel it.

GARY: You mean...? Really? *(Scott nods.)* Nice. Wanna?

SCOTT: I do.

GARY: My favorite two words again.

SCOTT: I do.

GARY: I do, too.

SCOTT: As if it were yesterday when we first said it.

GARY: I do.

SCOTT: I do.

GARY: I do. *(Gary leans forward and kisses Scott.)*

END OF PLAY

(As a reminder, a reduced royalty rate is available, either for individual plays or for a package of six to eight plays. For performance licensing rights, please contact the playwright at www.gregoryfletcher.com)

Stairway to Heaven
a short play
a drama

by Gregory Fletcher

CAST OF CHARACTERS:

ELISA, female, 17 years old.

GIL, male, 16 years old, Elisa's brother.

TIME: 2000.

Published by Dramatic Publishing in their anthology *35 in 10: Thirty-five Ten-Minute Plays,* www.dramaticpublishing.com and by Back Stage Books in their anthology *The Kennedy Center American College Theater Festival Presents.*

Premiered in New York City at Manhattan Theatre Source, produced by Gary Garrison, directed by Janice Goldberg, featuring Ari Butler and Allison Goldberg.

Winner of the National Ten-Minute Play Award from the Kennedy Center American College Theater Festival, where it workshopped with director Cathy Plourde, featuring Julie Miller and Ryan Bethke, and with director Jon Royal, featuring Kaitlin Yikel and Brian Watkins.

SETTING: The carpeted stairway of a middle class family home.

AT RISE: GIL, wearing a dark suit, is lying down on his back. His sister, ELISA, also dressed in dark colors and wearing a skirt, starts down the stairs. Her hair is pinned up in the messed-up look.

ELISA: Get up. *(No response)* I said, get up. Now!

GIL: So go.

ELISA: Like, I'm in a skirt.

GIL: Like, I'm gonna look? Gross.

ELISA: You're sixteen, of course you'll look.

GIL: In your dreams.

ELISA: Shut-up. Why don't you go up to mom so she can see how wrinkled your suit's getting. You should iron it.

GIL: And you should brush your hair.

ELISA: It's supposed to look like this, you creep. Move.

GIL: Just go if you're going.

ELISA: If you look, that's sexual harassment, and sexual harassment leads to sexual abuse, and statistics show that one out of five women are sexually abused by a family member.

GIL: I can't believe you're quoting your term paper to me. That is so lame.

ELISA: I got an A plus on that paper. Gil, enough, if you don't move, you are so dead meat.

GIL: Two deaths in one week? Doubt it.

ELISA: Please. Go see mom.

GIL: I'll see her when she comes down.

ELISA: I don't want her to be alone.

GIL: She's probably dressing, let her be.

ELISA: She's dressed, you're dressed, we're all dressed. Dressed and waiting. *(Sighs)* And waiting. Go on, at least while I'm making mom and me a cup of tea.

GIL: Oh, la-de-da, so adult. When did you grow up all of a sudden?

ELISA: When do you think? *(Gil looks away.)* She needs you.

GIL: No, his...when I had to go up for his dress shoes, for the funeral home...his closet...I could...you can still...

ELISA: Smell him? *(Gil agrees.)* So come down with me; I'll make you your first cup of la-de-da tea. You'll like it.

GIL: No.

ELISA: What?

GIL: Too many...the photo magnets on the refrigerator.

ELISA: Oh. Well, you can wait at the dining room table.

GIL: His chair. Waiting to be pulled out.

ELISA: The living room?

GIL: The recliner. His impression.

ELISA: Still on the cushion, yeah. The backyard? Never mind. The hammock. Even in the garage. His car.

GIL: I could feel him on the steering wheel.

ELISA: Then go in your room, at least you're safe there. I'll call you when it's ready. *(Gil doesn't move.)* In your own room?

GIL: Every trophy. Every ribbon. He's there, cheering me on.

ELISA: For someone who's dead, he sure is all around. *(She finally gets it.)* Except here.

GIL: So go. Scram. *(Elisa doesn't move.)* Elisa, I don't need your permission to be here.

ELISA: Look, Gil, I know you're upset. We're all upset. But no need to...I'm just saying, when things start changing around here—

GIL: Yeah, duh, they already have.

ELISA: I mean it, lose the attitude.

GIL: Stop talking down to me.

ELISA: F you.

GIL: You're using the f word?

ELISA: It was a letter.

GIL: Used in a complete sentence with a subject and verb.

ELISA: I didn't use the word.

GIL: And of all days, I can't believe you.

ELISA: It was a fucking letter.

GIL: Oh my God!

ELISA: I didn't...stop, you made me.

GIL: I should wash your fucking mouth out. *(Gasps in shock.)* Oh my God!

ELISA: You watch it!

GIL: I didn't mean it!

GIL & ELISA: I don't want mom to hear that kind of language.

GIL: Jinx, you owe me a Coke.

ELISA: Gil, you're gonna have to grow up. And fast.

GIL: Oh, like you're my authority figure now? My role model?

ELISA: Well, I am the eldest, and it only makes sense that—

GIL: By a year, big deal. I'm the only man of the house now.

ELISA: Don't think so. It's mom, dope.

GIL: Wrong equipment. Do I have to explain it to you?

ELISA: You can't even say the word.

GIL: Mom is not the man of the house and neither are you.

ELISA: Yeah, well—

GIL: Yeah, well, what?!

ELISA: *(They take a breath and calm down.)* If you really want to be the man of the house, then go see mom. Being the man means putting others first.

GIL: I just want to get this over with. When Howie Levy's dad died, they didn't drag it out with viewings and services. He was in the ground the next day.

ELISA: They don't believe in embalming.

GIL: You don't even know the Levy's.

ELISA: They're Jewish. It's a Jewish thing.

GIL: Oh. Well, makes more sense. I think when you die, you should get to be dead.

ELISA: *(Carefully)* Billy should've been invited.

GIL: Billy? Why...I mean, he...he's not that close to dad.

ELISA: To you. Special friends and loved ones...to comfort us in time of...oh, relax, no reason to clam up.

GIL: I just don't know why you think...I mean, it's...if—

ELISA. You're very close, you gonna deny it? Come on, Gil, when mom and dad went away with the church group, I know you guys—

GIL: It was a bath; we were in and out.

ELISA: Morning, noon and night? Please, if you weren't my brother, I'd think it was pretty hot.

GIL: Why do you bring this up like you got some power hold over me? You don't.

ELISA: Because you're gonna...you're gonna need someone special, you jerk. To confide in, to cry with, to get through this. And since you don't let me in...I can't even think of the last time we shared something important...really talked together.

GIL: *(Finally admitting)* Did dad know? Me and Billy?

ELISA: Why not? He's totally up on things.

GIL: *Those* things? No way, he's a Republican.

ELISA: Only financially. I mean, down deep, he's practically a hippie. He plays Led Zeppelin. Played. Whatever. I'm sure he was bound to talk to you about it.

GIL: What he was bound to talk about was how Eddie's too hands-on with you.

ELISA: At least we're out in the open.

GIL: Yeah, too open. Like we haven't all seen?

ELISA: As in mom and dad?

GIL: No, as in the entire neighborhood.

ELISA: Liar.

GIL: And he doesn't respect women.

ELISA: What do you know about it?

GIL: I know it's not right. You should respect yourself more.

ELISA: You, too. I hear you'll experience a huge relief when you come out of the closet. Like a heavy burden lifts from your shoulders.

GIL: Write a term paper on it, why don't you. You're just too scared not to have a date for the prom.

ELISA: Like you're gonna ask Billy to *your* prom?

GIL: Like you need a boyfriend in order to feel whole?

ELISA: Be proud of who you are.

GIL: Practice what you preach.

ELISA: Preach what you practice!

GIL: Elisa, enough.

ELISA: Homosexual shame is so twentieth century, get with it!

GIL: Hold your voice down.

ELISA: Alright. I'll talk to Eddie about it. When you talk.

GIL: That's the last thing mom needs right now.

ELISA: She can handle it. We can all handle it. As long as you're...you're...you know, playing it safe. Are you? Playing it safe?

GIL: Are you and Eddie? Playing it safe?

ELISA: Yes, dad, we are. Are you and Billy? *(No response)* Well?

GIL: Yes, dad, we are. We're not stupid, you know.

ELISA: Okay...I'm relieved. Good.

GIL: Yeah. Me, too.

ELISA: Cool.

GIL: So.

ELISA: Dad for each other then? On an as needed basis?

GIL: People would shit if I brought Billy to the prom.

ELISA: That's what people do. They shit. *(Gil takes Elisa's hand.)* You've got Dad's hands, you know. Throw your hand open, palm up.

GIL: *(Opening his hand.)* Weird, huh?

ELISA: Do it again? *(Gil opens his hand again.)* Identical. *(She takes his hand, and they sit holding hands for a good long moment.)*

GIL: Good. Okay.

ELISA: Okay what?

GIL: *(Standing and buttoning his jacket.)* I'll be up with mom. How do I look?

ELISA: Like the man of the house.

GIL: Yeah, you too. *(Gil exits up the stairs. Elisa exits down the stairs.)*

END OF PLAY

(For performance licensing rights, please contact Dramatic Publishing at www.dramaticpublishing.com.)

The Briefs

Know Theater

See as many plays as possible. Read as many as possible. Read books on playwriting as well as biographies of playwrights. Take classes in theater history and play analysis. (For the debate regarding the spelling of theater vs. theatre, please see Needed Vocabulary.) Push yourself to learn as much as you can. Realize that playwriting is a craft, which is why the spelling is "playwright" and not "playwrite." As with other craftsmen, playwrights have a toolbox to assist them in their art, many principles of which have been passed down through the centuries.

Writing from pure instinct will not give you an original voice; it will only deprive you of a vast wealth of knowledge that will assist you in building, writing, and revising plays. And when instincts run dry or when ideas are at a loss, the toolbox of principles will give you clues how to keep the writing moving forward. Writing blindly may work for the first draft, but true playwriting is more about the rewriting and revisions. Writing the first draft is the easy part. Shaping it into a well-crafted play that can withstand time and multiple productions will determine whether or not you're a playwright for the ages.

Only when you possess an understanding of craft can you choose to ignore advice, break conventions, and bend the rules as best serves your vision. But only when it's a personal, thoughtful choice; never from laziness or ignorance.

Participate with theater every chance you get, especially when in school. If you're not cast at auditions, don't just lay low for the semester. Volunteer, get involved, and learn every aspect of production. Assist the director or stage-manager, crew, prompt, run a light or sound board, learn how to sew, build a flat, help with the poster and program; the list is long and endless. Knowing theater completely will feed you invaluable information for writing plays.

When registering for classes, besides playwriting and play analysis, choose acting, directing, design, stage-management, theater history, and literature. One aspect of theater informs the next and will help guide your writing to a sense of stage worthiness, ready for the collaborative process to begin.

When possible, study art appreciation, music appreciation, psychology, religion, world culture, and its many histories. Travel whenever you can. When out of the U.S., attend theater. When home, attend theater tours from visiting countries. Performances in foreign languages will allow you to see theater in a brand-new way.

All that you experience will inform your writing. Therefore, never stop educating yourself. Be hungry to attend the next production and read the next play. Commercial or Not-For-Profit, professional or community/educational, rave reviews or panned, experience it all. Seeing what doesn't work is just as valuable as seeing what does. Every production is a learning opportunity.

Investigate discount tickets. The more you save, the more you can see. If you have a student I.D., 'Student Rush' offers discounted tickets, sold either when the box-office opens on the day of the performance or two-hours prior to curtain. 'General Rush' offers discounted tickets for the general public, also sold either when the box-office opens on the day of the performance or two-hours prior to curtain. Student Rush can be found in many Broadway theaters, but isn't consistent in any regard. It's up to the individual production to decide whether or not they offer student rush or general rush. A lottery consists of a limited number of discounted tickets offered two hours prior to curtain with a drawing of names. Student Rush, General Rush, and lottery can be found in major theater cities. Info regarding which theaters offer such discounted tickets can be found on Playbill.com.

No student ID? Take a night class so you can get one. Also, don't forget about standing room, volunteer ushering, and the numerous organizations that offer discounts and comps when tickets are available. In NYC, and other big cities, look for Audience Extras, Play-by-Play, Theater Extras, TheaterMania Gold Club, etc. Search the web, inquire at the box-office, and start seeing theater on a weekly basis. Only then will you write and profit as an informed craftsman.

The Producible Short Play

Just as any playwright can learn how to write a more producible play by knowing how a play is produced, the playwright of short plays can do the same by understanding how short plays are produced. Most short plays, also called ten-minute plays, are produced in compilations that consist of eight to nine plays. If five are produced in the first act, and four are produced in the second, plus an intermission and slight pause in between each play, the audience will experience a very full evening of theater. There are also festivals of short plays that continue for a full day (or weekend) or that change the lineup every two to three performances. Whichever way the collection is produced, shorts must co-exist with each other.

A short play is rarely fully realized with its set and lighting designs, because who can afford so many individual sets? What backstage can store that much scenery? Shorts are typically produced with either a unit set that works for all the plays (with minor adjustments) or an empty stage that allows each play to add the barest of essentials: a couch, a table, two chairs, a door frame, a desk, a rocking chair, etc. Rarely will the audience leave the theater admiring the scenery, the special effects, or the sense of spectacle. For a short play to win over the audience, it must rely on the quality of its writing, directing, and acting. Therefore, shorts with high scenic demands and expectations will most likely land in a rejection pile.

Similarly, the lighting plot for an evening of shorts will need to accommodate the full lineup of plays. For the playwright, this translates primarily into being able to distinguish between stage right (SR) and stage left (SL), as well as up stage (US) and down stage (DS). If you're lucky, you might get to isolate center stage or request one light special per play: a footlight, a leafy gobo, a specific down light or color, etc.

Since all the actors must share dressing rooms and a greenroom, try to keep the cast of characters to its barest essentials. Theaters with little backstage space must coordinate a very tight schedule of where the actors can prepare. While one group is performing on stage, the next is waiting backstage in the wings. The next two are in the greenroom, and the ones after that are in the dressing room. Even actor call-times may be staggered, especially for the actors performing after intermission.

There are always exceptions to the rules, but besides not requiring large scenic and lighting demands, as well as large casts, be careful not to require too big of a mess. Of course, it's possible the short that culminates with a food fight can end act one and be cleaned up at intermission. Or it's possible that the play that requires a large pyramid of Barbie dolls can open act two so that the props can be set during intermission. Keep in mind that the more your short play requires, the harder it will be to co-exist with others. Therefore, the less likely it will ever get staged.

Another performance arena for producing short plays is in acting and directing classes. As mentioned in the Introduction, a short play stands on its own and doesn't require further reading or explanations for the actors or audience. A short play has a beginning/middle/end, and therefore the character arc usually has more development. When a short play ends, there's a sense of completion, rather than a scene that depends on the next scene, and the next, never attaining a sense of completion until the final curtain.

With classroom productions, the scenic and lighting elements are even more limited than usual. More often than not, there are no lights at all, and scenic elements are limited to various rehearsal cubes and props.

There are usually more females than males in a theater class, and—not too profound, but as a nice reminder—students tend to be between the ages of 15 and 25. Despite the fact that student actors are accustomed to playing age, drama teachers are in search of short plays that feature age-appropriate characters and female roles.

Combining live music on stage with a performance can be thrilling and theatrical; however, most short play compilations are showcase performances, meaning no one is paid a salary. Finding actors, directors, and playwrights to showcase their work without compensation is much easier than finding a musician who will agree to do the same. (Unless of course you're producing at a school.) It would be a shame to end up in the rejection pile solely because of a stage direction that describes a flute player moving in and around the action.

In order to practice the craft of playwriting, a playwright must get produced. The experience obtained in a rehearsal room, participating with the collaborative process, will no doubt make a playwright stronger for his or her next play. By mastering the short play, many submission opportunities will consider your work. (Not commercial theater, but rather Equity Showcase, Community, and University Theater.) Producing an evening of shorts can be more profitable than producing one full-length play. More plays equal more cast members, which equal more audience members, which equal more box-office dollars.

While you're waiting for your big commercial theater break, writing short plays will help the emerging playwright prepare for the longer venture of writing one-acts and full-lengths. Ultimately, it's the new, vibrant full-length play that will launch a playwriting career. Yet, many talented playwrights continue to wait for the sun to shine on that new day. Until then, short plays will help hone your craft of playwriting and actually make you feel like a working playwright.

Short Play Vs. Sketch Vs. Scene

Many submissions for short play consideration are actually not plays at all, but rather sketches. Both short plays and sketches are around ten pages; both have characters, dialogue, staging, and design elements. Both can be funny, with the biggest laugh coming at the end; however, the story structures are quite different.

In a sketch, the structure is based on an idea (usually a funny one), which then is riffed upon, time and again, for the length of the sketch. The structure isn't developing forward and changing (a beginning/middle/end), but rather remains in place, circling the main idea. A sketch is similar to a jazz band where each member takes a solo. Each solo riffs off of the main melody and returns, and the next soloist riffs and returns, and so forth. The solos can go in any order, just like the riffs within a sketch. One riff (or beat) does not determine the next. Often they can be interchangeable, with the biggest laugh saved for the end.

If the structure of a sketch were to be diagramed, the funny idea would be at the center with a circle around it. Then each beat riffs out and returns, as if outlining the petal of a flower coming off of the carpel, the funny idea. By the end of the diagram, the story structure of a sketch resembles a bird's eye view of a full flower.

One of my favorite sketches of all time is SNL's "Debbie Downer" (along with "The Spartan Cheerleaders" and "The Culp Family Musical Performances," many of which were written and/or supervised by the gifted Paula Pell). The main idea (the center of the flower) is that Debbie is such a downer. Each beat shows just how well Debbie can bring everybody down and suck the joy from the room. Because the writing and acting are so funny, we're continually delighted with Debbie Downer's company.

By the end of each sketch, however, things are pretty much the same as at the beginning. Even from sketch to sketch, as it serializes, the sketch is not about forward development but about riffing off of the central conceit—Debbie Downer. She's been to Disney World, to the Academy Awards, to a birthday party, a wedding, a Thanksgiving meal, and to many other locations and occasions, but Debbie remains the same from one sketch to the next because her fans expect her to remain the funniest downer around.

To illustrate the structure of a sketch (from memory, so forgive any slight variations), Debbie has gone to Disney World with friends and they're eating breakfast at Mickey's Jamboree. With enthusiasm, her friends order everything from Mickey's waffles to Goofy's pancakes to Pluto's steak & eggs. When the waiter turns to Debbie for her order, Debbie can't help but remember the devastation of Mad Cow disease and how it ravages the brain. As if signaling the end of a beat, the first petal of the flower, the sound cue plays Wah Wahhhh. The second beat begins with a friend announcing that Tigger hugged her at the hostess station and, as an adult, who knew it would make her feel so very happy? Debbie recollects how poor Roy of 'Siegfried & Roy' hugged a tiger once, but it didn't turn out so well. Cue the sound effect: Wah Wahhhh. As Debbie's friends discuss which ride to do first, the third beat, the big Thunder Mountain Railroad is recommended, which reminds Debbie of a recent train explosion in North Korea and whether or not the truth of the accident will ever be accurately revealed. Wah Wahhh. Pluto comes over to the table for a group photo and just as Debbie snaps the camera, she depresses everybody with the memory of her two-year stint at Children's Hospital. Wah Wahhh.

The following petals (beats) that complete the flower diagram consist of Debbie wondering about terrorist attacks, heat stroke, and the recent telephone call from her doctor: "It's official; I can't have children." By the end, everyone has had it with her, and they rush off to try to enjoy themselves, leaving Debbie warning them to slather on the sunscreen to protect from melanoma.

"Debbie Downer" entertains us and makes us laugh throughout, and that's the point. One should no more expect a sketch to be a short play than expect a short play to be a sketch. They're apples and oranges, not meant to compete. In fact, they're even presented in different venues. Short plays are performed in a theater; sketches are performed in a comedy club or on a TV show. There was a time when sketches appeared on stage. In variety shows: vaudeville and burlesque. But today, a short play is directly related to a one-act and full-length play, rather than a sketch.

The structure of a short play is based on the same three-act story structure as a one-act and full-length play. Some writers believe the three-act story structure is only for realism and the well-made play, but I disagree. Structure can be found in non-linear plays as well as absurdist, surrealist, and magical realism—even Greek tragedy.

Structure is not style; it's a crafted method of storytelling. Despite a play's length (short, one-act, or full-length), the diagram of its three-act story structure starts as a flat line and then angles upward as it moves forward with its development, upward to illustrate conflict and tension (verses a flat line that illustrates no pulse, no life). The line continues upward through all three acts until it reaches the climax and then trails off at the end.

The three acts of story structure are not the same "acts" that are performed at a performance on either side of an intermission. Or the three acts with two intermissions, and so forth, which are found in many classic plays. The three acts of story structure guide the playwright to divide the short play into a beginning/middle/end, whether there is an intermission or not.

Each act develops forward, away from where it began. Very quickly, somewhere near the beginning of the play, a point of attack takes the play from general to specific. A dramatic question is asked and the world of the play is interrupted or changed. Often, too, the protagonist is identified.

The journey of the play develops forward with at least two turning points that move the play from act one (the beginning) to act two (the middle) to act three (the end), whereupon the climax is earned, the dramatic question is answered, and the stasis of the play's world either returns to normal or creates a new "normal." The turning points that force the play into new territory cannot exist without development. Act three cannot exist without the development of act two, and act two cannot exist without the development of act one.

If needed, the play ends with a quick dénouement, which brings everything to a close.

To illustrate forward development, here's a description of the short play, *Stairway to Heaven*, the last play of the collection from the first half of this book.

Act One: On a stairwell in a family home, a teenage sister picks a fight with her teenage brother. Clearly, they are both estranged.

Come to find out, it's the day of their father's funeral, and the eldest, Elisa, is trying to take charge by barking orders at Gil, who's not having any of it. Their bickering, regarding who's the new man of the house, escalates. When Elisa hears herself saying, "Being the man of the house means being there for your family," she tries to do just that with Gil, which changes the stasis of their world.

Act two begins (the middle section) with Elisa reaching out to her brother, wishing that Billy had been invited, a subject that's never been discussed. Gil feigns confusion, but Elisa continues: "Special friends and loved ones, to comfort us in our time of ... and since you don't let me in—I can't even think of the last time we shared something important, really talked together." She persists and goes a step too far, causing Gil to lash back with his own harsh truths: "What Dad would've minded was how hands-on Eddie is with you in public." Shocked to hear that anyone knew of her and Eddie, Gil confirms, "The whole neighborhood sees it." They continue pushing buttons and talking about things their father was bound to bring up if he had lived. Finally, a truce is achieved, which causes the stasis to change again.

Act Three begins, (the third and final section), as they admit they can be dad for each other, on an as needed basis. They realize they've been living without each other and that they do truly care for each other. By settling down and sitting with each other, Elisa sees her dad's hands in Gil's. "They're identical," she says. Gil sees it, too. She takes his hand, and it's the first time they've actually connected in years. In the final moment, at the climax, they come together and share a new calm and connection. They are no longer estranged.

Unlike longer plays that take more time to slowly introduce the characters and world of the play (as well as sub plots), short plays tend to jump into the point of attack right away. The protagonist is established, and a dramatic question is asked: will these estranged siblings stop bickering and find peace with each other? Elisa becomes the protagonist because she's more actively involved. She starts the bickering, continues it, and then causes the turning point that moves the play into act two. Later, after the truce, she's the one who sees her deceased father in the hands of her brother, and she reunites with him to bring about the climax of the play, which answers the dramatic question. Without Elisa, the play would not have taken place or developed forward. She's the one being brave enough to reach out for a stronger relationship. Granted, she doesn't figure out how to attain her goal until act three, but in the end she causes their relationship to go from estranged to reunited.

The revisions of a play edit out small talk, tangents, and any dialogue that doesn't develop the play forward. Because a beginning/middle/end must be covered within ten pages, editing focuses on deleting words to its barest essentials, isolating three distinct acts from one another, and reaching the climax by page ten, the latest. With a sketch, revisions simply tend to replace dialogue with funnier dialogue, and beats with funnier beats. Although don't be fooled by the word "simply," there's nothing simple about writing laughs. Comedy is some of the hardest writing to accomplish. In sketch writing, the comedy is more joke-based with funny punch lines. With short plays, the comedy can come out of the action of the characters, their needs, and situations.

Picking a suitably sized story for a short play is important. Often, the play will let it be known what length it needs to be, so it's possible a first draft of a short may turn into a one-act or full-length play. When considering a suitable story for a short play, examine whether or not a beginning/middle/end can be fully realized within ten pages. Can the dramatic question be posed and answered in such a short time?

A sketch offers a half dozen or more beats of a funny idea; the short play develops forward by three acts (beginning/middle/end), and therefore includes at least two turning points and a climax, which answers a dramatic question. When you can identify such building blocks of structure, it's easy to tell the difference between a sketch and a short play. Please don't confuse the two, or pass one off as the other.

Whether you refer to the three parts of story structure as acts, beats, or beginning/middle/end, the forward development has three distinct sections. If there are only two acts, or beats, or a beginning and end, you've written more of a scene than a play, and just as a short play is not a sketch, a short play is not a scene.

A scene can be revised into a short play with further development, or perhaps it's not meant to be a short play, but rather a scene within a longer work. A scene often develops only by one step forward at a time. A scene typically ends with a turning point, which then leads to the next scene, and to the next, and so forth. A scene does not usually have the forward development of a three-act story structure with a beginning/middle/end. A scene belongs within a larger play and usually does not stand on its own.

Similarly, the arc of the protagonist develops over the entire play rather than by the end of one scene. Presenting a scene by itself usually leaves the characters with little forward development, and leaves an audience wanting more. It's very rare that a scene leaves a sense of completion. A scene is intended to be one pearl in an entire string of a pearl necklace. Not until the end of a play can the entire necklace be viewed as a whole.

Playwriting Vs. 'Stenography'

Playwrights should refrain from sitting down too soon to write. A funny line of dialogue or a clever exchange between characters may pop into your head, and the 'stenographer from within' jumps to the keyboard as if not to miss a single word.

But there's a difference between being a stenographer and a playwright. Jumping into writing dialogue quickly may seem like playwriting, but if you don't apply the craft of structuring, then you're simply transcribing the voices in your head, and hoping it will resemble a play in the end.

On rare occasions, the play may 'write itself' during the first draft. If not, however, the power of understanding craft and applying its principles allows you to avoid being a slave to intuition. As a craftsperson, you should be able to identify issues within your play, anticipate problems, and refine the choices that will best serve your play.

Applying craft means different things to different writers. It can mean keeping the play in your head and thinking about it until you can no longer hold it inside. It can mean dwelling, considering, pondering what if this and what if that. It can mean journaling about back-story, family trees, and character histories. It can mean reading and researching about the world of the play, about a prominent subject, a historical person or time, specific community or dialect, etc.

When I'm thinking of a new play, I think of it as if I'm planning a road trip. What provisions might I need? I wash the car, vacuum the interior, fill up the tank, and bring along a map. Even if I don't want to choose exactly how I will arrive at my final destination, I give myself a few signposts to keep my writing on track.

Even accomplished playwrights have plays that are uncertain how to end. Perhaps they jumped into the car without knowing their final destination? No GPS, no provisions, no gas? Which might explain why some plays wander around and end without a sense of completion. Clever situations and witty dialogue can keep the play moving for a while, as well as the gun in the drawer, but sooner or later the audience in the backseat will realize the driver has no clue where he or she is going.

I've heard playwrights say, "I write to see why I'm writing; I write to discover; I write for the thrill of the ride." If he or she has a grasp on structure and craft, then absolutely, voyage ahead. After the first draft is discovered, the craft of principles and structure can be applied to the rewrites. However, for those with less experience, why not at least think about where you want to end up by the climax of the play? If you can see the target, it's easier to hit.

The map for a road trip is the equivalent to an outline for a play. How many details exist on the outline are up to you. Maybe the map won't be opened once, and the final destination will be reached with perfect timing. But then again, what if it's not? Relying solely on instincts and creative juices to guide you can leave you stranded on the side of the road. Thinking about the structure of your play will save a huge amount of time with revisions as well as with abandoned plays. For me, such discipline and planning can actually be freeing rather than confining.

I don't outline every step of the journey, but I don't drive without a map either. I try to find a happy medium. I agree that there are many discoveries to be made while writing and revising. Such discoveries are often the joy of writing. However, if I know my road trip is starting in Dallas, Texas and ending in Washington, D.C., I need to question why I'm veering south toward New Orleans. If I don't have a map (outline), I may not even realize I've gotten off course.

Even so, turning around and getting back on the 'right' road doesn't have to be an immediate choice. First, examine the journey to New Orleans to decipher whether or not the side trip serves the play. If so, then by all means follow the discovery. But if it becomes clear New Orleans is a self-indulgent tangent, not serving the play as a whole, then the outline will quickly get the writing back on path.

For writers who plan their final destination but little else, consider giving yourself a few signposts to help guide the writing. Signposts act as turning points, which will help aim the writing toward the final destination: the climax of the play. At the very least, signposts will help keep you from wandering around blindly and reaching your page limit way before its time.

Before getting specific about signposts, let's get specific about turning points. Typically, they do one of two things. A turning point either changes the stasis of the scene, which then propels the play into new territory; or, the turning point changes the action, bringing a beat to a close, which then propels the writing into a new beat, scene, or act. Either way, the play is propelled into new territory, continuing to move forward, developing plot, character, action, surprises, mystery, etc.

A turning point also allows the writing to remain specific and focused. If you're writing without a guide, it's possible to be too general, repetitive, and one note. When you construct turning points to change the stasis and/or action, your writing is guided to specific new territory and objectives. Constructing at least three distinct turning points promises three different parts to your play, beginning/middle/end, three beats, or acts.

In *The Nine-Month Fix*, there are several examples of turning points. When Lou and Steph are interrupted from the newspaper incident by a telephone call, the stasis changes, which allows Steph to melt and become a different person as she speaks to her mother on the phone. When the call ends, the former stasis returns so the newspaper incident can be brought to an end. The turning point that brings the beat to a close is due to action. Steph exposes Peggy's secret note to Lou within the newspaper, confirming their extramarital affair. Steph then creates a plan to end it, bringing the beat with Peggy to a final close. When Lou agrees that he understands, "Yeah. Loud and clear," the beat reaches its cap, its conclusion, and moves forward to something new.

Further turning points include getting Lou to apologize, which propels the action toward exposing how Steph became pregnant, which propels the action to dealing with her mother's involvement, which changes the stasis of Lou's and Steph's relationship, which propels the action to solving what will become of the baby, which leads to the climax of the play when Steph's water breaks. By the end, she has successfully changed this negative violent experience into something positive, which saves her future and family situation.

The signposts I consider before sitting down to write dialogue are the following:

Inciting Incident: The specific incident that causes the play to come to light. The Inciting Incident occurs anywhere prior to the beginning of the play up to the point of attack.

Point of Attack: A moment that occurs early in the play that brings the general world to a specific one, where the protagonist is identified, and a dramatic question is asked. Answering the dramatic question defines the journey of the rest of the play.

Act One Turning Point: Either a change in stasis or action that propels the play into its second third, (its middle section or act two).

Act Two Turning Point: Either a change in stasis or action that propels the play into its final third, (its end section or act three).

Crisis Decision (if needed): When the protagonist makes a crucial decision that triggers the climax of the play.

Climax: The ultimate turning point in the play, usually the most dramatic, which provides an answer to the dramatic question and brings about a completeness to the journey.

Dénouement (if needed): Tying up any loose ends and bringing the play to a close.

(See Needed Vocabulary for further definitions.)

To illustrate the signposts, see how they apply for the play *Roast Beef and the Rare Kiss:*

Inciting Incident: A genuine mutual attraction and former fantasy of the possibilities of a relationship between Alan and Paula, occurring prior to the beginning of the play.

Point of Attack: The tender, lovely, sexy kiss between Alan and Paula, occurring in the opening moment of the play.

Dramatic question: will this romantic first kiss lead to a loving relationship and future for this couple?

Act One Turning Point: Dee enters; the stasis shifts to reveal that Alan's and Paula's spouse are in the next room, the kitchen, cleaning up the dinner dishes. Alan and Paula are no longer a first date/first kiss possibility, but rather two halves of two heterosexual couples, cheating on their spouses in the very next room!

Act Two Turning Point: Alan and Paula are left alone one last time to figure out how their discovery will play out.

Crisis Decision: They decide not to act on the kiss.

Climax: Alan and Paula pair up with their partners for the viewing of the film, and the stasis shifts to reveal that they are two homosexual couples.

Answer to the Dramatic Question: No, the kiss between Alan and Paula will not move forward; the couples will remain as they are.

Dénouement: There will be longing at what might have been between them, but the subject won't be acknowledged or mentioned again.

The signposts used in writing *Roast Beef and the Rare Kiss* allow me to keep the three acts (beats or beginning/middle/end) focused and specific. Because of the signposts, I know that act one must come off as a first date, a first romantic kiss. Therefore, the dialogue must reflect innocence, naïveté, and inexperience.

When Dee enters, and it is assumed that she is Alan's wife, act two becomes a very different act than the first. The innocence and naïveté are gone. The action between Alan and Paula, despite their genuine romantic kiss, becomes aghast about cheating on their spouses in the very next room. The dialogue includes stuttering, pretending, blaming, and rejoicing that they weren't caught. And making sure it never happens again.

When the spouses leave to get napkins and split the popcorn, leaving Alan and Paula alone once again, act three begins with paranoia, whether or not their spouses suspect anything. Alan and Paula fantasize that the only way their being together could become a reality is if they moved away and started over. They question why the kiss took place in the first place and confirm their complete love and satisfaction with their spouses.

A crisis decision is understood between them as their spouses reenter and join them for the start of the film. At the climax of the play, a stasis turning point reveals that the two couples are not heterosexual, but rather homosexual, giving us a new perspective as to what just took place on stage. The dramatic question is answered, and the very short dénouement brings the play to a close.

Because of the signposts, the play has three distinct acts and includes development over much covered ground. The signposts keep the writing focused, which informs specific choices for writing dialogue.

Some writers are under the impression such signposts are only the building blocks for realism. But I disagree. Similar structure can be found in many genres of plays, from the Greek tragedy *Oedipus the King*, written by Sophocles around the year 429 B.C.E., to Samuel Beckett's *Waiting for Godot*, to most of the successful plays that withstand time.

Here are the signposts applied to *Oedipus the King:*

Inciting Incident: The second plague ravages the city of Thebes.

Point of Attack: As requested by Oedipus, Creon returns from the Oracle and reports that the plague will only end when the murderer of the former King Laius is discovered. Oedipus accepts the challenge.

Dramatic question: Will Oedipus be able to discover the former king's murderer? A case that's been closed for years? And by doing so, will he be able to save the city of Thebes for the second time?

Act One Turning Point: In questioning Tieresias, the local soothsayer, Oedipus pushes him too hard for answers, whereupon Tieresias accuses Oedipus himself of being the murderer of the former king. This changes the stasis of the investigation.

Act Two Turning Point: A messenger arrives from Corinth with the news that the father of Oedipus has died, which pushes Oedipus into darker territory via information shared by the messenger.

Crisis Decision: When Queen Jocasta realizes the true identity of her husband, she begs him to end his investigation. Even though she promises heartache and destruction to come his way, Oedipus refuses her advice and chooses to continue his investigation.

Climax: Oedipus discovers not only that he is the actual murderer of the former king, but also that King Laius was his birth father and Queen Jocasta, his birth mother. He then discovers that his actions have caused his wife/mother to hang herself, and in his shame at not wanting to see how others look upon him, Oedipus blinds himself.

Answer to the Dramatic Question: Yes, Oedipus discovers the murderer of the former King Laius and saves Thebes for the second time.

Dénouement: Creon becomes king, Jocasta is mourned, Oedipus says goodbye to his children and is ostracized from the city of Thebes. The plague has lifted, and the city is returning to normal.

A stenographer records the words that are spoken and heard. The stenographer is not a craftsman, but a recorder of voices. While it may be true that playwrights hear voices, listen, and write character dialogue, we are also craftsmen who create and build stories, assemble plot points in a telling order, and show the action of high stake intentions. Once we build the foundation for our play to exist, only then should the characters be allowed to speak and be transcribed.

The Character's Vocabulary

Writing too soon not only affects the structure of the play, but also the dialogue. When a playwright becomes a stenographer, recording the characters' words before their time, the words are rarely specific enough, and often sound as if they're coming from the same person—the playwright.

Perhaps you've seen (or rather, heard) a play where all the characters speak exactly alike? The cast of characters has the same vocabulary, the same wit, the same quick pace, and the same sentence structure. When dialogue is the last thing you commit to paper (or screen), the language becomes more specific, and such specificity within the dialogue will clearly define each character's individual voice.

You are the God of your play's world and, therefore, you should know everything about your characters from birth until their age in the play. Sometimes, it's not possible to hold all of the specific information in your head. Organizing your thoughts will help differentiate your characters and their vocabulary. I call the following chart Character Creation. (Don't be overwhelmed by the many aspects to specify. Certainly, you could easily fill out the following in regard to yourself, so why not for your characters?)

Character name:

Childhood nicknames:

Adult nicknames:

Gender assignment:

Gender orientation:

Age:

Date of birth:

Place of birth:

Place of childhood home:

Mother's maiden name and family roots:

Father's family roots:

Parent's religion:

Childhood church affiliation:

Parent's politics:

Medical issues:

Physical appearance:

Scars:

Current self-description:

Current wardrobe:

Adult church affiliation:

Adult politics:

Elementary school GPA:

Middle school GPA:

High school GPA:

Trade school:

College educated (where/major/minor/GPA):

Grad school (where and what):

Sexual orientation:

Sexual activity:

Career goals:

Current job:

Survival jobs:
Total Income:
Bank accounts and totals:
Pets:
Hobbies:
Cultural events attending:
Sports:
Secrets:
Meaningful relationships:
Children:
Grandchildren:
Circle of friends:
What friends say about character:
Renter or Homeowner:
Car (make/yr/condition):
Charities supported:
Music collection:
Other collections (stamps/trading cards/autographs/etc.):
Prized possessions:
Alcohol/drugs consumption:
Diet:
Weaknesses & vices:
Addictions:
Dreams/goals:
Eccentric habits:
Criminal record:
Recurring nightmares:
Real life fears:
Turn-ons:
Dislikes:
Favorite color:

Heavy baggage:

Outlook on life:

When first creating a character, your instincts and given circumstances of the play will help guide you. You can also learn a lot about your characters from research. Above all, listen to your head and heart, journal about the world of your play and its inhabitants, and fill in the specifics on this chart as the answers make themselves known. You'll discover more as you write the first draft. Sometimes the answers change; sometimes the list isn't complete until the play is done. The more specifics you know for each character, the more specific the vocabulary will be.

Fill out the Character Creation list for each character and let the specifics inform each and every spoken word.

Dialogue Isn't Talking

When it comes to dialogue, think of a toddler crying. The passionate cries are its way of communicating, because words have not yet been discovered. Besides the usual "goos," "gahs," whimpers, and giggles, the toddler doesn't passionately cry until it needs something, which summons the caregiver, who works through the list of possible problems: Hungry? Wet? Thirsty? Wants out of the stroller? To be held? Needs to be put down for a nap? Is the sun blinding? Until the toddler's needs are met, the cries are a matter of life and death.

This image reminds me not to commit a character's words to paper (or screen) too soon. Dialogue is the last thing I do when writing a play. Wait for your characters to cry out passionately for what they want before assigning a word.

Acting is action, drama is doing, and dialogue is both. Dialogue is never just about talking; it's always about dramatic action. Or, depending on your teacher's vocabulary, there may be other words used for a character's dramatic action: goal, intention, objective, task, or action. All mean the same thing: a character trying to accomplish something specific. No small talk, no chatting, no telling or describing the objective, just a specific goal to attain (or fail to attain) by the end of the beat/scene/act or play.

Even when dialogue is intended to sound like small talk, it must have a needed intention behind it. A female character may talk about the weather with another female character, not for the sake of the weather being described, but because she knows her husband's having an affair with this woman. She therefore speaks about the weather as she tries to control the conversation, in order to resist saying anything about the affair.

Most playwrights understand that characters want something, but the crying toddler reminds us that simply wanting something is not always enough. For example, wanting to say "hi" to another character at a bus stop isn't enough. The want should have high stakes. The objective cannot be frivolous, irrelevant, or unmotivated. Find the need behind every action, and then make the need great. Instead of wanting to say "hi" to someone at the bus stop, what if it's been months that the character has been trying to introduce his or herself, and now the other person standing at the bus stop is there with luggage. Saying "hi" becomes extremely important because, today, it's now or never.

Let the crying toddler remind you that wanting something is always about needing something extremely important. Let the objectives cry out passionately.

Emotion is Sweat

Despite the fact that audiences love to cry, and actors love to emote, playwrights should be wary of dictating tearful moments just for the sake of tears.

Emotion was made crystal clear to me in an acting class at Columbia University, taught by an extremely gifted director and professor, Bruce Levitt. A runner at the starting line of a race has one objective: to be the first past the finish line. The gunshot is fired, and the runners are off. The character's goal (or action, dramatic action, intention, objective, or task) is what he or she is focused on for the entire race, trying to win first place.

Because of the runner's focus, determination, and hard work toward attaining the goal, the runner begins to sweat. The sweat equals the emotion of a scene. Sweating isn't something the runner is trying to do or manipulate; it's a response to the action. The race is not about the runner's sweat any more than a scene is about the emotion. When emotional moments do not have a foundation of dramatic action, the emotion often turns sentimental, untrue, and self-indulgent. When emotion is a response to the dramatic action, it will hold weight, value, and never appear gratuitous.

Speaking of gratuitous, onstage emotion is like nudity. It's not something to cover up or of which to be ashamed. But then again, gratuitous nudity stands out as mere titillation and completely unnecessary. If emotion is not truly needed to move the action forward, then don't dictate it. Let the director and actors discover it within the rehearsal process. When nudity is needed, grounded, and natural, it's art. When it's gratuitous, it's pornography—and that's another medium altogether. Let it be the same with emotion.

Fill Up the Trunk

Howard Stein was one of the most important theater educators of my life. I'm very proud to have been in his handpicked first class at Columbia University, where he was Chair of the Hammerstein Center of Theater Studies within the School of Arts from 1982 to 1991. We had a similar passion and appetite for theater and later when I began teaching, it became very clear I was a Howard Stein protégé. Our friendship continued until his passing almost thirty years later. "Filling up the trunk" is a Howard Stein philosophy, and in his honor, I share his inspiration.

When a student of Howard's finished a play, he expected another to begin right away. Even when one was in rehearsal, he'd ask, "Are you thinking about the next one?" He never wanted anybody to stop writing until "the trunk was full." He'd seen too many playwrights put all their time into one play and not have much else to show. "There will come a day," he said with his usual enthusiasm mixed with warning, "when a play of yours hits, and the next day the inquiries will begin. What else have you got? Do you have a comedy? Do you have a two-hander? Do you have a family drama? Do you have anything epic? Do you have anything no one else has read before?" His point was, if you don't have anything else to show, you're missing a major opportunity to move your career forward.

Even if a second play was done, it was still the same reaction: "Fill up the trunk." If a student became too cocky and responded, "The trunk is full," Howard shot back, "Then get a bigger trunk."

Most producers and theaters are on the lookout for the next flavor of the month. When a playwright receives a good review, a small window opens when producers may approach. "You never know how long anyone will remain interested. If you have to put them off so you can finish the next play, they might be onto the next emerging playwright by the time you're ready." Howard understood momentum. "When your wave hits, you need to be able to ride it for as long as possible."

"Filling up the trunk" is a reminder to be prepared for when producers suddenly become interested. If one production can lead to the next, and then to another—careers can take off.

Formatting the Manuscript

Formatting plays on the page can be confusing because there's no official 'standard' format. In fact, the format can differ from east coast to west coast, and within the various proprietary scriptwriting software programs. Search the Internet for samples. (Don't copy the formatting from published plays; they usually have their own, specialized format. Play publishers try to get as many words onto each page as possible, because the fewer pages to print, the cheaper the cost.)

The format I prefer consists of a left margin and two tabs. It couldn't be simpler. The dialogue goes on the far left margin (with a 1.25" margin). The parenthetical goes at the first tab (an inch or 1.1" in from the dialogue). The character name goes at the second tab, (at 2.75", just left of center, depending how long the character names are).

Note the difference between the parenthetical that exists within the dialogue and the parenthetical that exists between two characters' dialogue. The one within dialogue has no extra spaces before or after, and it gives clues to the actor on subtext or action. The second one between characters' dialogue has a space before and after the parenthetical and describes stage business.

Formatting example from *Not Tonight*:

BILL
(Opening the box and taking out a slice)
This wasn't my idea. I didn't order it.

BOBBI
Oh, look, your favorite. Extra mushrooms. How you torment me!

(She exits. Bill picks off the mushrooms from
his slice and leaves them in the box. After a bite,
he moves to the front door, opens it, and returns
to the couch.)

BILL
Not hungry?

ROSS
Sometimes, it's best to wait.
(Bill hands him the second bottle of beer.)
So. Any improvement?

I'm not a fan of italicized stage directions in a playwright's manuscript. For a published script, which includes the formatting within this collection, I understand that italicized directions are the norm. Because the words are more compact within a published script, italicizing helps to differentiate the stage directions from the dialogue. In a playwright's manuscript, however, I prefer the font style of the stage directions to be normal and inside parentheses. Some writers squeeze their stage directions onto the same line as the character's name, or on the same line with dialogue. I prefer the parenthetical to be on a separate line.

Some playwrights start their stage directions at the centerline and continue to the right side of the page. Originally, this was very west coast. Today, formatting is no longer regional.

The formatting I prefer is from around the 1970's and back, when playwrights still used typewriters. My great aunt and uncle, Matilde and Theodore Ferro, were playwrights who also wrote for radio ("Lorenzo Jones and His Wife Belle"), live television ("Robert Montgomery Presents," "Somerset Maugham Presents," etc.), and later taped television in Los Angeles ("Leave It To Beaver," "Patty Duke," "Peyton Place," "My Three Sons," and the original "Guiding Light," etc.). I was given many of their manuscripts, along with manuscripts from their close friend George Sklar, and it's this format I use today.

At the top of each new scene, there are two additional descriptions: Setting: plus description, and on the next line: At Rise: plus description. The descriptions for Setting and At Rise line up with the character names, which are not centered but rather at the second tab, which makes for a nice clean line down the page.

Whichever formatting you use, stay consistent throughout the manuscript. When writing a short play, know that none of my plays within this collection are longer than ten pages (not including the title page and the cast list page). For further discussion, please see Short Play Vs. Ten-Minute Play in Needed Vocabulary.

All in the Revisions

Writing the first draft only happens once. Believe it or not, that's the easy part. Now comes the hard part: rewriting. Revision will either make or break your play. There might only be a few drafts, and, if so, congratulations! Or a dozen drafts might be necessary. Each play will have its own demands, and like a parent with a child, you must stay and work with the play until it's successful enough to be sent out into the world.

When it comes to revisions, don't jump in right away. Let some time pass. Waiting to revise can be very difficult because excitement and enthusiasm declares that it's the best play you've ever written in your entire life. Nevertheless, put it away and wait at least a few weeks. Even a month. And no peeking! Or, why not start another play and when you get to the end of the first draft, put it away, and come back to the play that's been waiting?

Revising without fresh eyes is ineffective because the closer you are to the play, the harder it is to see. As with every parent of a newborn who asks, "Isn't she the most beautiful baby you've ever seen?" Later, when you read your first attempt again with fresh eyes, you will realize the true answer about all first drafts: no, not exactly! Until you have fresh eyes, love is blind. So serve your first draft well by putting it away.

The time apart will guarantee a positive rewrite. With fresh eyes, you'll see things that are not clear, that you got wrong or left out, or that need more development or explanation. Not to mention typos!

When enough time has passed, try the following:

Examine the first line of dialogue. Realize you only get one first line, so try to make it special rather than clichéd or irrelevant. Then do the same for the last line of dialogue. Again, you only get one final line; make it worthy.

Next, closely examine each character's dialogue, one character at a time. As if examining an individual character arc, read one character's dialogue from the first word to the last. Skip all the other dialogue and stage directions. This will bring about a fine-tuning of revisions. First, it'll become quite evident how active (or not) a character is in each scene. If the character is a protagonist, remaining inactive or passive is something you'll want to revise. Tangents, where characters veer from specific intentions, can also be easily identified and eliminated with this method. Most importantly, vocabulary can be isolated from the other characters and closely examined. If you have a character who often says, "My goodness, you don't say," it's doubtful you'll want another character to use the same expression. Such details can easily be missed when reading the entire play straight through, but if you stick to one character's dialogue, their specific vocabulary becomes crystal clear. Such an exercise will allow you to tweak the vocabulary and sentence structure so that each character has an individual voice. It will be obvious when all of your characters curse in the same manner. Or when they interrupt and finish each other's thoughts in the same way. Or when they all have the same witty comebacks or absurd sense of humor. Reading one character's dialogue straight through clearly signals when words do not solely belong to that character, but rather to the playwright.

Next, consider the 5 W's: What, Why, Where, When, and With Whom. What is the character doing? (Meaning trying to achieve.) Why is the character doing it? (Meaning motivation.) Where is the character doing it? (Meaning setting.) When is the character doing it? (Meaning year, season, and time of day.) And with whom is the character interacting? (Meaning relationship.)

The 5 W's inform the words a character chooses. A character's dramatic action and motivation may remain the same as in the first draft, but did you fully consider if the scene is taking place in public or in private? In the frigid cold or the summer heat? Speaking with a lover or a teacher? A grandparent or a sibling? A customer or a beggar? No one speaks the same all the time. Exploring the five W's will help fine-tune the dialogue to a specific vocabulary.

As recommended by my friend and colleague, Jean Klein, also a student of Howard Stein's (from University of Iowa), examining the French Scenes can be very telling. See Needed Vocabulary for a full definition; however, a play is divided into acts; acts into scenes; scenes into French Scenes; French Scenes into beats; beats into moments. A new 'French Scene' is determined by the entrance or exit of a character. For example, *The Moon Alone* has a total of three French Scenes: 1) Precious and Samantha; 2) Precious, Samantha, and Val; 3) Precious and Samantha. By isolating French Scenes, you can more easily identify where the play loses momentum because of a lack of action. Also, when you become aware of the length of individual French Scenes, you'll get a strong sense of the overall rhythm and pace of the play.

Finally, read the work aloud. Hearing the dialogue read out loud will be very different than silent reading. And if you've been solely reading off your computer screen, print out a copy and read it through on paper. This will also make you see the words in a different way.

When the second draft is complete, ask a couple of friends to read and discuss it with you. Give them two or three weeks (or more) before hounding them for a response. Don't rush them because the time apart will be good for you. Based on their confusion, questions, and misconceived interpretation, you can head into a third draft.

Next, invite some actor friends to read the play out loud. You may ask, how do I get actors to come over to read a play? Easy— feed them! And most importantly, don't participate. Don't read a role, don't read stage directions, and don't direct. Just sit and listen. Maybe you'll want to invite a couple friends to listen as well. Hearing the words read aloud by actors is the most invaluable thing you can do for the revision process. Actors will lift your play to a new level. Afterward, their comments, moments of confusion, and reactions will lead to a fourth draft.

Next, you're ready for a larger reading, one with an audience of at least 25. Find a space to borrow or rent at a reasonable price. Hearing and watching an audience respond to your play is the second most invaluable thing you can do for a play's development. Don't just invite friends and family. Invite strangers, too, so the reactions aren't purely a love-fest. Sit in the back so you can easily watch the audience. Listen to how they respond and watch when they fidget.

If you do a talkback afterwards, simply listen to the comments. Do not defend your play or answer questions. Just respond, "Thank you, I'll consider it." If you have specific questions to ask the audience, do so. But again, only listen, don't debate or defend. The audience reactions will guarantee insight for another revision.

A note about notes: there will be people who'll read or hear your play and want to rewrite it. Listen to your gut to know when a note truly serves your play. If it doesn't, be courteous, give thanks, and let it go. The interesting thing to consider about bad notes is not the actual note itself, but where in the play the remark was triggered. Often, audience members don't know how to identify a problem but perhaps are identifying where attention needs to be paid. Even if the note is totally off-base, check out where in the play it was given, and re-evaluate that beat.

Optimistically, after five drafts, your play is ready to be sent out into the world. Rest assured that more revisions will come. If a theater becomes interested in your play, they may schedule their own reading, and then you'll most likely get notes from a dramaturg, as well as from the director of the reading. Then when the new audience hears and responds to the play, more revisions will occur.

Revising a play is a process. Trust the process. Develop patience and perseverance. Listening and considering. Knowing when to say, "No, thank you, that's not my play." When in doubt, breathe, listen, and obey your head, heart, and guts.

Participating in the Rehearsal Process

In theater (unlike TV and film), writers occupy a powerful position because we own the copyright to our work. In TV and film, writers write "for hire," and the producing company owns the work, which is why the pay is comparatively much greater. In theater, if a totem pole were to be carved to illustrate the levels of creative power, the playwright would be at the top, whereas in TV and film, writers would be near the bottom. The playwright has a great deal of say in who's hired to direct, design, and act. Also, any ideas, feedback, or improvised dialogue that comes from the rehearsal room may be used by the playwright without sharing any credit or royalties.

Despite the playwright's power, it is important to know the dynamics of the rehearsal room. The director runs the rehearsal like the captain of a ship. Trust that you have the power, and play the humble card. Above all, know that a playwright is always welcome in the rehearsal room. Or rather, permitted anytime he or she cares to attend. A playwright never has to wait to be invited or given permission to sit in on rehearsals. Having said that, a playwright should not interrupt the work the director is setting in motion.

In the first few rehearsals, during table work, questions may be addressed (depending on the director's ego) directly to the playwright: questions about dialogue, specific word choices, any confusion of character or stage direction, etc. Who better to answer than the original creator? When responding, simply state the facts from a writer's perspective. "When I was writing this moment, I was thinking this or I meant that." Do not give line readings to the actors. Do not dictate interpretation. The rehearsal room is a collaborative process, so don't treat anyone like a puppet. Stronger interpretations, a fresher way to achieve an action, or a funnier way to end a line may be offered. You would be foolish not to consider such well-intended suggestions by people directly involved in the play. Allow everyone to contribute because, in the end, your play will benefit.

When the actors are on their feet, it's a good time to sit in the back and listen. If you make a discovery and want to change dialogue or revise a scene, simply take notes and speak to the director at a break. The director will implement your changes as best serves the rehearsal. What's to be rehearsed and when, including the full rehearsal agenda, is solely up to the director.

Try not to be result-oriented. Don't forget that the director has four to five weeks to prepare the actors for a performance level. You may not see what you want in the beginning, but trust that the director knows how to get the actors where they need to be. The rehearsals are process-oriented, not result-oriented. If the director asks the actors a question they can't answer, don't offer the answer (unless called upon). Spoon-feeding the actors won't serve your play. Actors must be allowed to make discoveries and become a part of the interpretative process.

How do you know if you and the director are on the same page? Waiting until the rehearsal period may be too late. At your very first meeting, ask him or her to tell you the story. If irrelevant things or a different story are described from the one you intended, then you'll know this director is not the right choice for your play.

If actors stumble with dialogue, investigate those moments to see if there's a problem. Deleting extra words can make the dialogue cleaner, more economical, and less of a mouthful. If a particular line remains hard to memorize, sometimes, the incorrect way an actor memorizes a line is actually better. If you agree, you can officially approve it with the stage-manager and keep the credit for yourself. If you don't agree, however, and the actor continually gets the words wrong, or isn't paying attention to important punctuation, give line notes to the stage-manger, who'll pass them to the actor. Actors are expected to memorize dialogue word-for-word. Verbatim, to be exact. Paraphrasing is not allowed!

Once the playwright feels comfortable with the revisions of the script, take a break from the rehearsal process. In the same way that it's beneficial to put a first draft away, it's also beneficial to take a break from rehearsals. When you return, you'll have fresher eyes and ears, and potential improvements may become more obvious. You may notice not only small moments to revise, but also other issues: perhaps a scene is running too long for the balance of the act, or the overall play is running too long. The closer you are to the performance, the harder it will be to hear the moments that are crying for your attention.

If an actor with a question corners you, answer him or her, but stick to the facts so that you're not crossing over into the director's territory. Never approach an actor with any personal notes or direction. Problems develop when there are too many chiefs. If an actor disagrees with the director and wants you to get involved, don't. In private, you can tell the director that you agree with the actor's interpretation, but never manipulate the dynamics of the rehearsal room. Give your notes to the director, and let him or her decide how best to handle the notes. Some directors may want a playwright to give notes directly, but never assume until you're directed to do so. Directors will work as they see fit in the rehearsal room; rarely do they adapt to how the playwright wants to work. The playwright adapts to the director. In the end, if you don't like the way a director conducts a rehearsal process, then don't work with him or her again. It's always your choice.

Creativity is a fragile thing; no one really knows where it comes from. But, clearly, it doesn't take much to destroy a creative atmosphere. Judgment, tantrums, rolling of eyes, and any other kind of disrespect or insensitivity will be deadly. Negativity is the quickest way to stamp out creativity. Attending rehearsal should be a joyful process, where everyone's free to create and discover. No one strives to be incompetent or to produce unworthy work. Being a part of a successful theatrical event is everybody's dream. Be grateful to all in the room, especially those who are left out of the curtain call: the stage management team, the backstage crew, the office and front of house. Show your gratitude daily and help keep things productive and positive, because everyone is there to serve your play. If everything comes together, the success of your play will be replicated in theaters across the country. Even, perhaps, around the world. And you'll be back in the rehearsal room time and time again with new plays.

Try To Avoid

Avoid narration: Don't cop out and narrate. Allowing a character to stop the dramatic action of a play in order to explain things to the audience indicates to me that the writer couldn't find a way to dramatize the scene. Whenever I'm watching a performance, and a character talks directly to the audience, I instantaneously drop out of the world of the play and wonder, Who do they think I am? And why are they talking to me? If the answer's not immediately obvious, I have to assume the character's talking to me out of convenience, and immediately I stop trusting the playwright as a capable storyteller.

If a character must speak directly to the audience, think of it as a scene between two characters. Give the audience a character, obviously a silent one, but when the relationship between the two is clear, and the character needs to speak, then the dialogue becomes relevant and the farthest thing from narration. I've seen many successful examples where the audience is addressed as a classroom of students, a jury, citizens at a town hall meeting, etc.

Avoid reminiscing without dramatic action: Avoid easy, clichéd dialogue like, "Remember when we...." Or "I remember when you used to...." When both characters already know the information, yet rehash it for the audience's sake, it becomes heavy-handed exposition. Find an active, subtle way to introduce exposition and be sure the characters need to talk about it. If not, do without until you can find the appropriate place.

Avoid spoon-feeding: Announcing to the audience what a character's objective is will come off as lazy. Dialogue like, "What do you want from me?!" Or "What are you trying to do here?!" Or "Can't you see, I'm trying to warn you!" Even though these things may be said in real life, such obvious dialogue is too simple, on-the-money, and heavy-handed. When I hear, "What are you saying exactly?!" and "You don't know what you're doing, do you?!" I immediately have the same thoughts about the playwright.

Likewise, avoid stating the theme in an obvious manner. Spoon-feeding the audience is insulting. No one wants to be talked down to, especially as the climax approaches. If the audience doesn't get the point, look for a rewrite, instead of imposing a set of CliffNotes on the dialogue.

Avoid sitting still: Avoid seating two characters on a sofa or at a table for a long period of time. Find reasons why they need to get up on their feet and move. Allow the forward development of your play to move the scenes and travel the stage.

Avoid staging the play: Allowing your play to move doesn't mean dictating the staging. Some published scripts include stage directions from the original blocking, but realize such notes often come from a stage manager's promptbook rather than from the playwright. The playwright does not need to describe the angle in which a character crosses to the desk. What's needed is that the character crosses to the desk, not crosses stage right to the desk.

Instead of blocking your play within the parenthetical, trust that the director will stage your play and allow your stage directions to illuminate the stage business that is vital to the storytelling.

Avoid designing: In much the same way that you should avoid doing the director's job, also avoid doing the designers' job. Certainly, list whatever is needed on stage, but no need to dictate the floor plan. Whether or not the desk is stage right or stage left, let the set designer do his or her job and figure out what best serves the play. Theater is a collaborative art form, so allow others to contribute.

Avoid pretentious stage directions: "The play takes place now" isn't very helpful. Are we supposed to search for the year of copyright? Or for the year the play was first produced? What about in ten years? Will the play still take place now? If you do not wish to set an exact year to the play, then avoid mentioning it at all. No need to be esoteric.

"The clothes and hair styles are now and then." When exactly? "Then" includes many periods you may regret seeing on stage. Always be specific.

"She speaks and gestures as one does when down and out." Not helpful, unless you're aiming for clichés.

"His boyish charm is neither." It may work in a novel, but not in a play.

Naming characters as "A" or "1" or "Woman" may work on occasion, especially from celebrity playwrights, but more than not, it's only pretentious. Even with a play that features two life long friends who never refer to each other by name, they still have names. They still know each other's name.

Of course, there are always exceptions to the rules, and stage directions are supposed to be helpful clues to those who are studying your play and mounting a production. Aim to be helpful rather than pretentious.

Avoid constant plotting: Even though great stories must be told and plot points well arranged, avoid abandoning characters, relationships, and the living/breathing hearts on stage. Heart and connections are the main ingredients of a play. Pure plotting makes for a dry, heartless play. See The Last Word on Principles.

Avoid low stakes: A character's objective, what a character is trying to achieve, must be highly needed. If the ramifications of not achieving the objective are not high, then revise the stakes. Aiming for high stakes makes for urgency, which usually creates electricity on stage.

Avoid the mundane: Why waste time on writing a play that's not relevant or important? If it's not essential that you tell this story, or share these human beings, the audience will sense it right away. If you don't care, the audience won't either. So only choose subjects that matter to you. Consider writing about what makes your blood boil? What makes you belly laugh until it hurts? What scares you more than anything else? What makes your heart pump fast? If you could do one drastic thing in your life, what would it be? Etc.

Avoid the rush: Try to avoid sending your play out before its time. Literary offices rarely reread a play when it's revised. The piles of scripts they have to consider are endless so use your one shot wisely. Plus, remember, love is blind. Whenever a new play is completed, it's normal to think that it's the best play you've ever written in your entire life, and this is the play that will guarantee a successful reputation and career. Time apart from our loved ones will always give us fresh eyes toward our work. Time apart will help us see our bundles of joy with clarity and reality.

The Last Word on Principles

Principles that are passed down from one generation to the next are tools to be used as needed. They're not a formula that guarantees the perfect play; nor are they a recipe for success. Be leery of any book or instructor that purports to give a list of rules that will write your play in two weeks flat. Or that guarantees to produce a commercially-viable property. As much as I value the principles (which I continue to learn), playwriting takes far more than knowledge of principles. Because plays show and tell stories of the human spirit, plays—first and foremost—must contain heart. Without heart, a play cannot breathe, feel, or connect. Without heart, plays tend to be dry, technical, and rarely come to life on stage in a meaningful way.

Writing with heart means letting down walls and listening. It means daring to write your truths without denying what's passing through the creative consciousness to the page. Writing with heart means allowing the human beings and relationships within your play to be just that: living, breathing, feeling, human beings, with warts and all, filled with the human spirit. If we solely rely on principles, our plays will end up too much in our head. Which isn't to say there isn't room for intellect in a play, but not to the extent that the heart of the play is forsaken.

How does one let down the walls and listen? It's different for each and every one of us: meditation, focusing on the here and now, yoga, long walks, exercise, being among nature, the arts, journaling, giving yourself time to reflect, etc. For me, it's usually as simple as getting enough sleep, eating a healthy diet, asking questions, walking on a beach, listening to the ocean, giving of myself to others, showing gratitude, and giving thanks. This is how I try to live life in order to keep the walls down and the ears open.

The creative process is difficult to understand. It's fragile and must be handled with care, respect, and gratitude. Just because you tap into it once doesn't mean it's guaranteed to follow you with each new play.

Tapping into creativity is a constant state of discovery. Think of each new play as a new baby. The birthing process and experience will rarely be the same because each new play will have its own needs and demands. What worked brilliantly for one play may not work for the next. As with babies and children, each one will have its own personality, and the playwright must accommodate its needs or there will likely be trouble.

The good news is that when you learn and store principles, they will be there for you when you need them. For more experienced playwrights, principles may not be called upon until the revision process begins. The first draft can be written purely from the heart, instincts, and discovery, as well as imagination, fantasy, guts, mystery, and anything else the creative spirit calls forth. Then, in the revision process, principles may be used like a checklist, which will inspire needed revisions. For newer playwrights, principles can be invaluable tools used from the very beginning of preparing to write a play. Think of principles like target practice. They help focus our ideas, and writing the first draft will be easier to complete when you have a goal and a climax for which to aim.

With principles, plays will no doubt improve and benefit from the wisdom that has been passed down throughout the ages. There's a sound reason why principles continue to be passed down from generation to generation: because they work. But only as an addition to a writer's heart and listening skills. Never as a replacement for the human beings and relationships on stage.

Search and Submit

The largest listing of submission opportunities and contests comes from the Dramatists Guild Resource Book. All members receive an annual copy, plus monthly listings within an email newsletter.

There are many listings of submission opportunities and, what with the ease of search engines, you'll be able to find more than you can handle with a single search.

On Facebook alone, there are countless groups and listing services. The same is true for Twitter. So many groups share the latest opportunities for submissions.

There are sites that, for a small annual fee, will send you submission opportunities on a monthly basis. My favorite is http://playsubmissionshelper.com/

There are numerous journals that will publish short plays. The more your plays are read, the more opportunities that may materialize for production. Search and submit.

Also, search and join writers' groups. Writers tend to share the latest news of submission opportunities with their cohorts.

When you submit a play, keep a spreadsheet of all your submissions. Indicate the date sent and to whom, and then return to the entry with the final outcome: accepted or rejected. Don't be afraid to keep a listing of rejections. The list will remind you how long you've been at it, and no one will ever be able to accuse you of being an overnight success. Many people believe that submissions are simply a numbers game. Statistically speaking, the more you submit, the more chances you have to be produced.

Every year there are new sites. Simply search and submit on a weekly basis. Remember, it can't be all about writing. You must give yourself a business day once a week or at least once every couple weeks. If your work is not being submitted, then how will you ever be produced? Doing business not only includes submissions, but also includes letters of inquiry, thank you notes or emails, and keeping people and social media apprised of your work.

Surviving the Biz

Beyond playwriting, consider the following life principles:

Delayed Gratification: When you're out of school, keep your monthly nut as small as possible. Too many talented individuals have been forced to give up a life in the arts because they needed a higher income for their monthly bills. There's no shame in moving on to a new career or life path, nor in wanting a car or a higher quality of life. Just be sure it's your choice and not forced upon you, because living in a state of woulda-shoulda-coulda may haunt you for years to come.

Until you find a new passion to replace your life in the arts, make some adjustments. Stop buying things with a credit card unless you can pay it off at the end of the month. Embrace frugality. Save as much money as possible, keep track of how much you earn and how much you spend, and pay off debts as soon as possible. The longer you can survive a life in the arts, the better for us all.

Just Ask: Creativity is fragile and difficult to fully understand. Where does it come from? Why do some tap into it more (or less) than others? Instead of waiting for creativity to come a-calling, summon its presence by asking a question. Ask any specific questions that need answers. Ask such questions aloud and frequently. My favorite time to ask is when I first go to bed. There's something special about this time of night. Ask, and wait for the answer to come back by morning. If not, keep asking until the answer arrives.

Getting into bed is also a great time to verbalize gratitude for all that took place throughout the day, and for all that's anticipated for tomorrow.

Ask and receive. Keep a pad of paper and a pen on your bed, or a recording device, because when you get the answer, you'll want to record it. Don't assume for a moment that you'll be able to remember it in the morning.

Patience and Perseverance: Playwriting and production takes time. Theater is very different from the music industry, where a song can be written in two hours and recorded the next day. And sometimes make a fortune shortly thereafter! A play can take years before finding a home for production and, worse yet, some wonderful plays may never find a home. It's not just about the writing. Most creative careers have a business side, too: schmoozing, making connections, sending submissions, following up, sending thank-you notes or emails, and when in doubt, continuing to do the work of writing. It's not talent that starts a career; it's timing and connections. Talent will sustain a career.

"Save the Drama for the Stage!": A good reminder that the only healthy drama is the kind that is rehearsed for the stage. Off-stage drama is only negative energy that ultimately crushes creativity. It shuts people down, causes walls to go up, and calls upon fear, paranoia, and insecurity. It keeps people from listening, contributing, and offering their best. Negativity is the number one enemy in the arts, as well as in life. Whatever you have to do to keep things positive, joyful, and productive, do it tenfold.

Keeping things positive takes a daily commitment. Negativity will sneak into your day every chance it gets: through gossip, jealousy, fear, and every other quality that connects to the ego. When you feel negativity interrupting your day, steer clear. Either physically move away or ignore it as best you can. Do not engage with it, because it will only snowball and grow bigger until it is out of control.

It's impossible to be both negative and positive at the same time. You can only be one or the other, so choose to remain positive. Pay negativity no mind. Or better yet, turn it around by saying or doing something positive.

I have a friend who says that whenever things get dark in life, turn on the lights. This reminds us that a choice is always involved. You can live in the dark or you can live in the light. Living in both, at the same time, is impossible.

The Definition of Success: Careful how you define success. A life in the arts is not usually a money-driven career path. It's more about the heart and passion. Success comes from doing creative work. Not that money can't arrive too, as well as Tony Awards and the penthouse view. But awards, money, and material goods are like icing on a cake. As my grandmother used to say, "Icing is pure sugar; it's not really that good for you."

My definition of success continues to change with time. Today, success is about living debt free, giving of myself to others, feeling a sense of joy and positive energy in my life, having good health, friends, and family. In other words, even though I welcome awards, recognition, and the penthouse view, I already feel successful with or without it.

Warming up: Musicians warm up before playing; dancers and athletes warm up before performing, too. Why not writers? Our instrument includes our body, mind, and heart. Before jumping to the keyboard to write, take a few minutes to prepare. Start with a few deep breaths: in through the nose and out through the mouth. Stretch your major muscle groups to help release tension. Sit still for a few minutes and focus on the five senses and living in the here and now. When you take the time to become grounded, calm, and stress free, you're building a solid foundation for creativity. Trying to write when you're hyper, tense, or distracted will only make for a unstable foundation. A five or ten-minute warm-up before writing summons the body, mind, and heart to focus and prepare.

Also, I warm up prior to teaching a class, presenting a panel, doing a reading of a play, going to an interview, even before going to bed. Warming up allows me to swat away the tension, distractions, and negative frequencies that have attached to my being throughout the day. Incorporate warm-ups into your life, two or three times a day, and see how it makes a difference in your writing and quality of life.

Needed Vocabulary

5 W's: The 5 W's help writers inform specificity to dialogue, action, and stage directions. Also, they help actors and directors inform choices of interpretation and staging. The 5 W's include What, Why, Where, When, and With Whom. What is the character doing? (Meaning trying to achieve within a beat.) Why is the character doing it? (Meaning the motivation; the justification.) Where is the character doing it? (Meaning the setting. Is the location of the scene in public or private? Is it interior or exterior? etc.) When is the character doing it? (Meaning the year, season, and time of day.) And with whom is the character interacting? (Meaning the relationship between the characters.) All will inform specific choices.

Acts, Scenes, French Scenes, Beats, Moments: A play is broken down into acts, then broken down into scenes, then broken down into French Scenes, then into beats, and lastly, if needed, moments. The playwright usually labels the acts and scenes, but leaves further scene breakdown to the director. A play must be broken down to study its structure, to analyze its parts and ingredients, and to create a rehearsal schedule.

There are two different kinds of acts: 1. A play (regardless of its length: a short play, one-act, or full-length) is written in a three-act story structure, meaning the structure contains a beginning/middle/end or acts one, two, and three. 2. A play is performed in acts. One, if there is no intermission; two, if there is one intermission; three, if there are two intermissions, and so forth.

Acts are divided into one or more scenes. Often the scene changes to another scene when the location or setting changes, or when the time of day/month/season or year changes.

When the playwright does not provide labeled acts and scenes, the play can be broken down into French Scenes. A new scene begins with the entrance of a character and continues until a character exits or until another character enters.

A beat lasts as long as a character's objective. A character tries to get money from a friend. The beat lasts until the character achieves the goal or not. By the end of the beat, the character will either be a winner or a loser. A second definition exists between musicians. How many beats are there per measure? Sometimes a playwright will use a stage direction (Beat) much like a musician. Meaning he or she wants the actors to wait a beat or pause. I refrain from using (Beat) this way because it can be misinterpreted by actors for a change of beats. Try to be as specific as possible. When a pause is needed, use the stage direction (No Response). Or (Stalling). Or (Refusing to answer). Give specific clues to the actor. Pauses come to life when there is action. The stage direction (Waiting for a response) tells the actor exactly what they're doing vs. (Pause) or (Beat). The inexperienced actor may simply stop and hold, which will stop the action completely.

A moment literally consists of a few seconds. The playwright might say, in the moment the two characters meet eyes, their attraction to one another is quite evident. Or, in this moment, the characters realize they are not strangers but old childhood friends. The director might say, in the moment where your hands accidentally touch with his, let's see that you're very fond of each other. Or, take more of a moment after he leaves to realize you'll never see each other again.

Action, Dramatic Action, Goal, Intention, Objective, Task: What a character is doing and trying to accomplish within a beat. The what of the 5 W's. By the end of the beat, the character is either a winner or a loser when it comes to what was achieved or not.

Activity, Stage Business: Physical activity that takes place on stage. If a character is sweeping the floor, it's an activity. Or polishing a piece of silver, setting the table for dinner, brushing a sibling's hair, rolling a cigarette, getting dressed, eating an apple, exiting the stage—these are all activities, as long as the activities are not objectives (or actions, dramatic actions, goals, intentions, or tasks).

Activity is at its best when it relates and parallels the dramatic action; i.e., when the wife is trying to hold it together emotionally and therefore reapplies her make-up. Reapplying make-up is an activity because it's not what the wife is trying to accomplish within the beat. Her objective is to put up a wall to keep her emotions in check—to put on a brave face. Therefore, reapplying make-up makes for the perfect activity because it parallels her action of trying to hold it together emotionally, putting up a wall, and putting on a brave face.

Antagonist: The character who gets in the way of the protagonist, creating conflict. The antagonist is the one pushing stumbling blocks in front of the protagonist.

Aside: When a character turns and speaks directly to the audience. If there are other characters on stage, they do not usually hear the words of an aside or see that the character is speaking to the audience.

Back-Story, Exposition: Information within dialogue that describes prior facts or information to the start of the play, or prior to the current scene. Often, the characters already know the information, but the dialogue is needed so the audience can be informed of certain facts and/or what's happened prior to the scene.

Be careful with imposing too much exposition within the dialogue because it will slow the action to a halt.

Character Arc, Character Spine: An examination of a character's dramatic action from his or her first entrance until the final exit. Think of each scene's objectives as a vertebra, and the character's complete time on stage as the spinal column. Such an examination is essential for the actor, director, and playwright to study.

Character Flaw: The human quality that brings about the character's downfall. For Oedipus, hubris; for Othello, jealousy; for Cyrano, self-doubt, etc.

Cold Reading: Implies that the actors are reading without any rehearsal. It can also imply that the reader has not seen the material before and is literally reading it out loud for the first time.

Conflict, Stumbling Block, Obstacle: A complication or problem that is pushed in front of a character, trying to trip him or her, and make their objective more difficult to attain. An obstacle is created so that a character cannot attain his or her objective too easily.

Crisis Decision: If needed, it's a moment late in the third act (of the three-act story structure) when the protagonist makes a decision that triggers the climax. (In *Oedipus the King*, when Queen Jocasta suddenly realizes the true identity of her husband, Oedipus, she begs him to end his investigation immediately. She promises it will only lead to heartache and destruction, but Oedipus refuses her advice and chooses to continue the investigation, which brings about the tragic climax and conclusion of the play.

Dash (—) Vs. Ellipsis (...) Vs. Slash (/): Use a dash at the end of a line of dialogue to indicate that the next speaker interrupts. Dash equals interruption.

Use an ellipsis within or at the end of dialogue to indicate the character is searching for a word but cannot quite find it yet. This ellipsis does not have a space before or after. Ellipsis equals searching for the right words.

The ellipsis (with a space before and after) is used within a one-sided telephone conversation to denote when the off-stage character is speaking. This ellipsis equals waiting while the off-stage character speaks.

Use a slash within the dialogue to indicate when the next character should begin speaking. It doesn't indicate for the current speaker to stop speaking or to quicken the pace. The dialogue is completed as written. Slash equals overlapping dialogue.

Dénouement: The final moments of a play, after the climax, when the story, characters, and any loose ends are brought to completion. Most short plays, because of the limit of ten pages, have a very short dénouement.

Dramatic Question: Usually asked with the Point of Attack, when the play goes from general to specific, and when the protagonist is identified. The dramatic question propels the journey of the play and is answered at the climax, which signals to the audience that the journey is complete.

In *Oedipus the King*, in response to the desperate citizens of Thebes, Oedipus inquirers what must be done to end the second plague that is destroying their city. The Oracle responds, the murderer of the former king must be discovered. When Oedipus agrees to investigate, he is identified as the protagonist, and the journey of the play begins. The dramatic question asks, Will Oedipus be able to find the murderer or not?

Dramatists Guild of America: A national organization that supports, advises, and brings together playwrights, librettists, lyricists, and composers. It's not a union because its members do not work for hire; we own the copyrights to our work. The Dramatists Guild offers legal advice, online biographies on their website, national conferences, the annual Resource Directory, round table discussions, a magazine, and numerous opportunities to meet and greet within the community. No matter what level you're at as a writer, joining the Dramatists Guild is in your best interest. Visit www.dramatistsguild.com.

Dramaturg: (British spelling, Dramaturge): An employed position at a regional theater or a freelance position. For a new play, the position involves an understanding of play analysis, playwriting, and offering questions and insights for pre-production revisions. In the rehearsal period, the dramaturg presents research and/or an information packet for all involved. The dramaturg observes rehearsals and becomes a third pair of eyes for notes. A well-balanced position that does not involve directing actors or dictating rewrites, it may require correcting an actor's pronunciation based on research, or offering cultural gestures or posturing that comes from research, etc. In production, the dramaturg may write an article for the Playbill and moderate post-show discussions with the audience. Visit Literary Managers & Dramaturgs of the Americas at www.lmda.org.

DS, US: When the director is staging your play and tells the actors to move upstage or downstage, up is toward the back wall of the stage, and down is toward the front edge of the stage, also known as the lip. These directional terms first came about in the Italian Renaissance when set designers were experimenting with forced perspective and actually lifted the back end of the stage, creating a raked stage. Walking toward the back wall was literally walking uphill, upstage.

Epilogue: Rarely used, a short, separate scene that appears after the climax of the play. The epilogue appears outside of the three-act story structure.

French Scene: A play is divided into acts; acts into scenes; scenes into French Scenes; French Scenes into beats; beats into moments. A new French Scene is indicated by the entrance or exit of a character.

Given Circumstances: Unchangeable facts within a play that are not up for interpretation. If a play states that the protagonist stutters, it's a given circumstance, not up for discussion with the actor. If four scenes are written to follow the structure of winter, spring, summer, and fall, it's a given circumstance despite any interpretation from the designers. If the mother makes an inappropriate pass at her son, that relationship is a given circumstance and cannot become a stepson or other relation. Some things are up for interpretation (like staging, pacing, subtext, the choice of furniture, clothing, lighting, etc.), but not with given circumstances.

High Stakes: Great ramifications for a character not achieving his or her objective. The higher the stakes, the greater the urgency, which can create electricity on stage.

Inciting Incident: What causes the play to occur? In *Oedipus the King,* the Inciting Incident is the second plague that ravages the city of Thebes. If it weren't for this plague, the citizens of Thebes would never have approached Oedipus for help. And therefore, the investigation of the former king's murderer would never have taken place. Without the Inciting Incident, there is no play.

Monologue: A long passage of dialogue for a character. Other characters on stage hear the words and respond, unlike with aside or soliloquy.

Motivation: The "why" of the 5 W's. (Why is a character pursuing that objective?) Identifying why a character is doing something. Justification. She's asking him for the time to see if he's wearing a wedding ring on his left hand. She's sitting down because she's feeling dizzy and doesn't want to fall over in public and cause a scene. He's wrapping leftover bread in a napkin so he will have something to eat later. There is motivation for everything we do in life. Justifying each choice, each decision is something everybody involved must consider.

Parenthetical: Where the playwright leaves clues for how to say the dialogue, found within parentheses, i.e., (Lying). Could also include dramatic action; i.e., (Trying to emotionally hold it together). Could also include stage business; i.e., (Ironing his dress shirt).

Point of Attack: Where the play goes from general to specific, when the protagonist is identified, and where the dramatic question is asked. Where the specific journey of the play is propelled forward.

Prologue: Rarely used, a separate scene prior to scene one, usually a short scene. The prologue isn't called scene one because it appears prior to the three-act story structure of the play.

Protagonist: The main character who is identified at the Point of Attack, who then becomes the primary focus of the main journey of the play. The protagonist is present all the way through the play, participates with the crisis decision and climax, and by the end of the play either achieves his or her super-objective or not.

Reading Vs. Staged Reading: A reading typically happens with a group of actors around a table. Each is assigned a character role, and one other person reads aloud the stage directions. If an audience is involved, the actors may sit in a row of chairs or stools facing the audience. Sometimes, they stand behind a row of music stands. The rehearsal time can go from one to three hours or so, usually enough time to read through the play one time and receive a few notes of direction.

A staged reading usually has actors up on their feet with scripts in hand, making entrances and exits so that the only actors in front of the audience are the ones in the scene. Other moments may also be realized with staging and direction; i.e., a kiss, a shove, or simple staging. The rehearsal time can go from three to twenty hours, spread across one to a few days.

Readings and stage readings are an extremely important part of the new play development process; however, established plays can be read, too. For example, if a play has already been produced and published, perhaps the reading or stage reading is a way of presenting possible future titles for an upcoming season, or presenting literature to a class or group.

Royalties: The process in which a playwright earns a paycheck for writing a play being produced. Many producers are under the false impression that royalties are waived for non-paying audiences. According to the Dramatists Guild and the royalty description, there is no differentiation between a paying audience and a non-paying one. Plays that are performed in front of any kind of audience require a royalty to be paid to the playwright. For me, the classroom is the exception, but others may disagree.

The royalty for a short play is cheaper than a one-act or full-length play, as it should be, since more short plays are required for a full evening of theater. Royalties for short plays are currently around twenty dollars a performance, which can still be expensive if eight or nine plays are being produced in one presentation. Especially since the royalties for a full-length play are around seventy-five dollars per performance.

Royalties are paid per performance. If a publishing house licenses the performance rights to a play, then a royalty is paid directly to the company. If the play is not licensed, then the playwright's agent (or playwright) should be contacted directly for further negotiations.

SL, SR: When the director is staging your play and tells the actors to move right and left, don't be perplexed when the actors move in the opposite directions. Stage Left and Stage Right are taken from the actor's perspective, when facing the audience. The director learns how to direct the actors in the opposite direction from the perspective in the audience.

Short Plays Vs. Ten-Minute Plays: My preferred term is the 'short play' because, for me, the art of writing a short play is in the pages, not the timing. I would rather be guided by a ten-page limit than a stopwatch that will change with each and every production.

Most people use the term 'ten-minute plays' but isn't it odd to read a submission request asking for ten-minute plays that run between eight and twelve minutes? Shouldn't a ten-minute play be ten minutes? I dislike the image of a producer glued to a stopwatch. If a play reads in ten minutes by the playwright, it doesn't mean it will do so at the rehearsal table with actors. And it won't remain the same time when the actors are up on their feet at a dress rehearsal, or in front of an audience with reactions of laughter and applause. Each production will have its own timing, and it's nearly impossible to write a play that adheres precisely to ten minutes. Certainly, I aim for ten minutes, but first and foremost I serve the play.

Any producer who forces a playwright to cut because of a stopwatch, or sacrifice a few lines of needed dialogue or a moment, is too business minded. He or she should focus on achieving extraordinary short plays vs. ten-minute plays that have been edited for the sake of time.

Using a standardized playwriting format, I recommend aiming for ten pages because counting pages is completely within control of the playwright. Once you bring in a director, actors, sound designers, etc., there are too many variables that are out of the playwright's control. A short play occupies ten pages or less.

Short Play Vs. One-Act Play Vs. Full-Length Play: Think of how many plays equal a full evening of theater. With a full-length play (with or without an intermission) only one is required, usually lasting at least 80 minutes. With one-act plays, which tend to run between 20 minutes and an hour, two to four plays are needed to make a full evening of theater. With short plays, around six to ten are needed. By the end of which, the audience should feel full, satisfied, and complete, ready to move on to a restaurant for a post-show discussion.

Soliloquy: When a character verbalizes his or her internal thoughts, usually alone on stage, thinking out loud; i.e., Hamlet's "To be or not to be" speech. If other characters are present, they do not usually hear the thoughts being expressed.

Stasis Disruption: In the early moments of a play, often occurring simultaneously with the inciting incident, without which the play would not take place, the normal world is altered and disrupted. The journey of the play that follows tries to return the world to its normal stasis or, by the end, creates a new "normal."

Turning points are brought about by either a change in character action or by a stasis disruption. If a couple is kissing at a dining table in a restaurant, and the man's wife approaches and taps him on the shoulder, the stasis changes.

Story Vs. Plot: The story of *Oedipus the King* has been told throughout the ages. The story remains the same in each new version, but what changes is the plot. When a writer decides to tell the story of Oedipus, he or she chooses which plot points to use and places them in a particular order. Even though the story is not original, the selection and placement of the plot points most certainly are. One writer begins the story when Oedipus is already King of Thebes in the middle of the second plague. Another writer begins when Oedipus is a teenager overhearing gossip about his supposed fate. Another writer begins when Oedipus is approaching Thebes suffering from the monstrous Sphinx during the first plague. Another writer begins with King Laius being cursed by the gods with the prophecy that his children will pay the price of his past crimes. There have been long and short versions of the play, contemporary and period versions, even animation, claymation, and puppet versions. All have the same story but different sequences of plot points.

Subtext: The true meaning underneath a line of dialogue. What is truly being said by the character. When "yes" really means "no."

When "I love you" really means "I want your money." When "Get out of here" really means "Stay with me, baby."

Super-Objective: A character's overall objective (or action, dramatic action, goal, intention, or task) for the entire play.

Survivor Job: A job that pays the bills rather than defines any career aspirations. Just because you're waiting tables to pay the bills doesn't mean you're a career waiter.

Tactics: Different ways a character can go about achieving the same objective (or action, dramatic action, goal, intention, or task). When one tactic doesn't achieve the goal, another tactic may be used. It's the same beat because the intention hasn't changed, only the way of achieving the goal. For example, the tactics of Oedipus to convince Tieresias to shed light on the former king's murderer could be as follows: first, he commends his years of service to the city of Thebes. When that doesn't work, Oedipus tries to win him over with compliments that flatter Tieresias for his god-given gifts. When that doesn't work, Oedipus asks as a personal favor, friend to friend. When that also fails, he tries to win him over by evoking his sympathy for the lives of the dying citizens of Thebes. Next, he bluntly demands what he needs from him, as king of Thebes. Finally, he threatens to punish him for his disobedience, which then finally elicits a response from Tieresias. All are tactics for achieving the same goal.

Theater Vs. Theatre: My drama teacher in junior high taught that "theater" (ending with the -er) was where movies were projected, and "theatre" (ending with the -re) was where live performance was produced. Not only did the two words have different spellings, but different pronunciations. "Theater" was pronounced "thee-A-der" and "theatre" was pronounced just as you might expect, but with a slight British accent.

Other explanations for the different spellings have come and gone over the years: "Theater" is the building where theatre the art form is performed. Or theatre is the French spelling of the German/English spelling of theater. Then Britain started using the French spelling to appear high-class, followed by the Americans, who didn't want to feel inferior.

Searching theater spellings within the League of Resident Theaters, most theaters in the USA use the -re ending. To me, maybe because I studied French in high school, theatre looks like a French word. Since I speak English, and because I try to curb any pretention on a daily basis, I choose to spell it with the -er ending. If I am working at an institution that spells it with the -re ending, I adapt with no fuss. Note, however, that many people who spell it with -re are not always as adaptable. If you are outraged and generate hostility for users of the -er ending, I'm guessing the problem is bigger than spelling.

Clearly, there are two camps regarding the spelling, and undoubtedly I'm in the minority. Even so, when you see how many legitimate leading theaters across the country use the -er ending, no one can question the high quality of theater or authenticity. Some of my favorites include American Conservatory Theater, American Repertory Theater, Dallas Theater Center, Guthrie Theater, Joseph Papp Public Theater, and Lincoln Center Theater, to name a few.

Turning Point: A turning point occurs when a beat comes to a conclusion; either the character has achieved his or her goal, or not. At such time, the action changes course. There can also be a turning point when the stasis changes. Larger turning points occur at the end of acts one and two, (within the three-act story structure), a climax to each act. Often, the climaxes of act one and two are simply called "turning points" so the term "climax" can be used solely for the end of act three.

Writers' Group: What a book club is for readers, a writers' group is for writers. Some specialize in a specific genre (i.e., playwriting, fiction, creative nonfiction, poetry, screenwriting) and others invite a variety of genres. Usually, the group meets between once a week and once a month. Depending on the length of the meeting, one to four writers will present a selection of their work, and a discussion of constructive criticism will follow. Sometimes, with plays and screenplays, roles will be assigned to the members of the group or volunteer actors will be brought in to cold-read.

Acknowledgements

Heartfelt thanks to Northampton House Press for their invitation and support, especially David Poyer, my editor. Admiration and thanks to Naia Poyer, who helped copyedit the text and designed the cover. Gratitude to my colleagues (and friends) who gave of their time, expert eyes, and response: Robert Antinozzi, Jean Klein, Kevin Oderman, and Sara Pritchard.

Thanks and recognition to my agent, Marta Praeger, at Robert A. Freedman Dramatic Agency in New York City.

Much appreciation to my employer (and colleagues) at CUNY – Kingsborough Community College, where I am an Associate Professor and Director of Theatre Arts.

Gratitude to the premiere producers of my short plays: Paul Adams, Gary Garrison, Janice L. Goldberg, Lyralen Kaye, and Kate Snodgrass, as well as the Maslow Foundation Salon Reading Series at Wilkes University, and its MA/MFA Creative Writing Program, Bonnie Culver, director. Also, thanks and admiration to my colleagues (and friends) at Wilkes University for their support, expertise, and inspiration.

Love and thanks to Tom and Carrie Fletcher for always opening their home to me to write, along with the great comfort of the Princeton, New Jersey Public Library.

Appreciation to the Grand Mayan Resort and Hacienda Trés Rios in the Mayan Riviera of Mexico for the escape and paradise, my favorite place to write.

Finally, whether in a writing class, workshop, or one-on-one mentorship, my teachers have been an invaluable source of insight, wisdom, and support. Many, I am happy to report, have remained life-long friends. With gratitude, I honor the following teachers and playwrights who have influenced my life and work as a writer:

Matilde and Theodore Ferro, my great aunt and uncle who were writers for radio, live television, taped television, short stories, novels, and plays. Brenda S. Prothro, my high school drama teacher, the first person to put a playwriting book in my hands and to produce a play of mine, formerly at Justin F. Kimball High School in Dallas, Texas. From the Department of Theatre at California State University at Northridge: Mary Jane Evans, George Gunkle, and Bobbi Holtzman. From the Oscar Hammerstein II Center for Theatre Studies within the School of Arts at Columbia University: Howard Stein, Bruce Levitt, and George Ferencz. During grad school fellowships, Mac Wellman at La Mama E.T.C., the National Playwrights' Conference at the O'Neill, and Brian Clark on his Broadway production of *The Petition*, directed by Sir Peter Hall, and starring Jessica Tandy and Hume Cronyn. During my time as a stage manager, I had the great fortune to be at the table with Edward Albee, Christopher Durang, Tina Howe, Steve Martin, and Anne Meara. In the English Department/Creative Writing Department within the Graduate School of Arts and Sciences at Boston University: Kate Snodgrass, Neal Bell, and Richard Schotter. In workshops at the Kennedy Center American College Theatre Festival: Nilo Cruz, Oskar Eustis, Gary Garrison, Gregg Henry, Arthur Kopit, and Marsha Norman. Other memorable workshops include Edward Albee, August Wilson, John Guare, and Robert McKee.

About the Author

Gregory Fletcher is a native of Dallas, Texas, a resident of New York City, a graduate of California State University at Northridge with a BA in Theater, a graduate of Boston University with a MA in Playwriting, and a graduate of Columbia University with an MFA in Directing. Off-Off Broadway playwriting credits include *Edenville, My Sister the Cow, Eight Times Around, Stairway to Heaven, Roast Beef and the Rare Kiss, Robert Mapplethorpe's Flowers*, and *The Moon Alone*. Regionally, these plays and others have been produced in Boston, Miami, Moscow (Idaho), and Provincetown.

Awards include the Mark Twain Prize for Comic Playwriting and the National Ten-Minute Play Award from the Kennedy Center American College Theatre Festival, and a first runner up for the David Mark Cohen National Playwriting Award from the Association of Theatre in Higher Education. Fletcher was a playwriting grantee at the Sundance Theatre Lab, a nominee for Outstanding Original Short Script for the New York IT Awards, and a national finalist for the Heideman Award and the Reva Shiner Comedy Award.

Fletcher's plays have been published with Dramatic Publishing, Back Stage Books, and *Wilde Magazine*. His essay, "The Sealed Envelope," is included in the anthology, *Being: What Makes A Man*, published by The University of Nebraska-Lincoln Gender Programs, edited by Jill McCabe Johnson. Check out www.amazon.com/author/gregoryfletcher.

Playwriting teaching credits include Bloomsburg University of Pennsylvania, Niagara University, Wilkes University, and at CUNY Kingsborough Community College.

For more, visit www.gregoryfletcher.com.

Other plays by Gregory Fletcher

<u>Full-length plays</u>:
A Port in a Storm
Bliss You
Cow-Tipping and Other Signs of Stress
The Darling Kids—the True Story
Edenville
Riddle of the Sphinx
Tom & Huck—Breakin' the Law
Uploaded

<u>One-act plays</u>:
Art and the Large Endowment
Bardo
Coke and Sympathy
My Sister the Cow
Underdeveloped Photographer

Northampton House Press

Northampton House publishes carefully selected fiction – historical, romance, thrillers, fantasy – and lifestyle and literary nonfiction, memoir, and poetry. Our logo represents the Greek muse Polyhymnia. Our mission is to discover new writers, and give them a chance to springboard into fame. See our list at www.northampton-house.com, and Like us on Facebook – "Northampton House Press" – for more great reading.

8484046

CPSIA information can be obtained at www.ICGtesting.com
Printed in the USA
LVOW06s1327270815

451782LV00005B/232/P